MEDICARE'S MIDLIFE CRISIS

MEDICARE'S MIDLIFE CRISIS

SUE A. BLEVINS

CATO INSTITUTE
Washington, D.C.

Library of Congress Cataloging-in-Publication Data

Blevins, Sue A.
  Medicare's midlife crisis / Sue A. Blevins.
    p. cm.
  Includes bibliographical references and index.
  ISBN 1-930865-08-2 -- ISBN 1-930865-09-0 (pbk.)
  1. Medicare--History. I. Title.

  RA412.3 .B56 2001
  368.4'26'00973--dc21

                                                    2001047325

Cover design by Amanda Elliott.

Printed in the United States of America.

CATO INSTITUTE
1000 Massachusetts Ave., N.W.
Washington, D.C. 20001

Contents

Acknowledgments

Understanding the complex and confusing Medicare program is a daunting task that has required an enormous amount of research and analysis. I am most grateful for my educational experiences at two of the nation's leading universities, the Johns Hopkins University School of Nursing and the Harvard School of Public Health. Faculty at those institutions provided me with the research skills, leadership ability, and confidence to challenge commonly held beliefs. Even those professors who may not have agreed with my philosophical beliefs of limited government and individual liberty nevertheless served well as mentors.

For the opportunity to learn about seniors' health care, I am grateful to the many patients to whom I provided nursing services in various settings, including nursing home, hospital, and home environments. I would like to thank the nurses, physicians, and health care executives who trained me in those settings both in the United States and in Canada. The experience and insider's perspective have been invaluable in understanding Medicare's impact on seniors.

I am grateful to the Institute for Humane Studies at George Mason University for its financial support. In 1997, I was awarded a Social Change Research grant to study the history of Medicare, its development, and its effects. This permitted me to discover important information not widely disseminated.

Many people encouraged me to write this book and assisted with its organization and development. In particular, Alice J. Rini, Associate Professor of Nursing at Northern Kentucky University, spent time during a sabbatical to help me investigate past and current Medicare issues. She contributed to the sections of the book regarding Medicare financing for physician education and prescription drug coverage. She also reviewed drafts and provided insightful comments. Naomi Lopez Bauman, director of the Center for Enterprise and Opportunity at the Pacific Research Institute for Public Policy, provided intellectual inspiration.

To Debbie Grady, I am most grateful for her excellent research skills and dedication. She discovered an extremely useful bibliography of newspaper articles covering Medicare during the 1960s. She helped compile and organize information from existing books and articles on Medicare. Jennifer Rogers and Arlo Pignotti also provided valuable assistance with locating and compiling historical documents. Christopher Middleton provided insightful comments on actuarial data. They all helped tremendously checking facts and proofreading.

I am grateful to Sheldon Richman, editor of *Ideas on Liberty*, for his editorial assistance and important feedback on the manuscript. Sheldon encouraged me to examine how American families used to rely on "sickness" insurance, which paid lump sums of cash when they became ill. This idea was extremely appealing as it meant individuals controlled their own money for health care.

Tom Miller, director of health policy studies at the Cato Institute, dedicated a significant amount of time reviewing drafts, making recommendations for timely updates, and obtaining comments from expert reviewers. Tom's significant recommendations contributed greatly to the empirical evidence referenced throughout the book.

To the many reviewers—colleagues, advisors, and friends—I am thankful for their insights and comments on the many revisions of the manuscript. Scot Plank; Robin Kaigh, Esq.; and Ed Hudgins, director of regulatory studies at the Cato Institute, were especially helpful.

Finally, I am extremely grateful for the freedom of speech that exists in the United States of America. Without this precious liberty, I wouldn't be able to reveal many unknown facts about Medicare— the largest single payer of health care in the United States. Those facts supply readers with the strongest reasons for heeding the message of this book.

Preface

If you pay taxes, sooner or later your life will be changed by Medicare. When you turn 65, you will have to enroll in Medicare's hospital insurance program or lose the Social Security benefits promised to you during your working life. Once enrolled, you'll be subjected to thousands of pages of Medicare rules and regulations dictating what types of health care are covered and what are not, how long you can stay in the hospital, and whether or not you can receive home care services. If you happen to require home care following a hospital stay, you'll be forced to share psychological, sexual, and financial information with the federal government as part of Medicare's new home-monitoring data collection system.

These and many other facts are not well known about Medicare—one of the world's largest medical programs, which spent more than $221 billion in 2000 and is expected to require $645 billion in federal general revenue subsidies over the next decade (between 2002 and 2011).[1] A Kaiser Family Foundation/Harvard School of Public Health poll found that 63 percent of seniors know only a little or nothing about Medicare and efforts to reform it. Seventy-nine percent of individuals under age 65 also admit to knowing very little or nothing about Medicare and the current policy debate.[2]

In addition, many Americans don't know that the program was created as part of a larger plan to create a government-financed national health care system. Incremental steps were taken in 1965 toward that goal, including the establishment of Medicare Part A, Medicare Part B, and Medicaid, the government program for low-income individuals of all ages.

This book explains how Medicare came about, and clarifies why Congress created three separate government health programs in the 1960s. Most important, it gives the reader an overview of how Medicare affects his or her life today and how it could do so 30 years from now. Using government studies, congressional testimony, academic journals, and other sources, I have compiled important facts and analyses that would be hard to find in any single place. Finally, this book provides guiding principles for helping Americans gain greater control over their own health care, and hopefully tax dollars, too. Whether you're already retired or still working, this book will provide you with a greater understanding of Medicare.

The book is organized into six chapters: Chapter One introduces the reader to Medicare and provides a broad overview of the program, including the current economic outlook. Chapter Two examines the historical debate and early efforts to implement compulsory health insurance in the United States. Chapter Three discusses Medicare's passage and early evolution, examining the political climate during the early 1960s. Chapter Four explores the important issue of whether government officials concealed the true costs of Medicare when the program was being debated in the 1960s. Chapter Five examines Medicare's impact on seniors' life expectancy, poverty rates, and health care costs since the program was enacted in 1965. Finally, chapter Six discusses key concepts to consider for Medicare reform. The purpose of this book is not to provide a detailed plan for reforming the Medicare program, but rather to explain how we have reached this critical point and outline basic principles for dealing with Medicare's midlife crisis.

Even as Medicare faces major financial problems in the years ahead, seniors will expect the program to cover more services, such as prescription drugs and preventive care. These competing pressures place unrealistic demands on Medicare. They need to be reconciled within the next decade before Medicare exhausts its claims on future taxpayers.

There is no more important issue than one's health. Hard-working Americans deserve to know the truth about the Medicare program, including its original purpose as well as its impact on the economy and the principle of freedom of choice. Americans of all ages are encouraged to familiarize themselves with Medicare, for only then will they be able to make fully informed decisions about reform. If we better understand the program's history, we can avoid repeating past mistakes and begin to transform Medicare in the 21st century.

Sue A. Blevins

1. Don't Know Much about Medicare?

Upon nearing age 65, John Pearson[1] went to his local Social Security office to apply for his retirement benefits. He was planning to recoup the Social Security taxes he had been paying his entire working life, but he had no intention of enrolling in Medicare. After reading many articles about Medicare, John understood how bureaucratic the program could be. (There are more than 130,000 pages of Medicare regulations.)[2]

John believed that, over time, enrollment in Medicare would increasingly diminish his ability to choose medical practitioners and would limit his choice of treatments. Also, the thought of dealing with a huge government bureaucracy regarding personal health care decisions at the end of life seemed intolerable. Even though he had been paying taxes to support Medicare since its creation in the 1960s, he decided that when he retired he would forgo joining Medicare and instead continue paying premiums for the private, high-deductible, catastrophic health insurance plan he had purchased through a professional association.

However, John was astonished at what he discovered the day he applied for his Social Security retirement benefits. He informed the office clerk that he wanted to apply for retirement benefits. The clerk proceeded to ask him for personal identification information, such as his full name, Social Security number, date of birth, and other information. The clerk then printed out a "personalized" form titled "Application for Retirement Insurance Benefits." That form included the following statement:

> I apply for all insurance benefits for which I am eligible under Title II (Federal Old-Age, Survivors and Disability Insurance) and Part A of Title XVIII (Health Insurance for the Aged and Disabled) of the Social Security Act, as presently amended.

The clerk then asked John to sign the application form she had completed in order to further process his request for benefits. He

1

paused because he knew that "Part A of Title XVIII" (in the above statement) really meant Medicare Part A (hospitalization coverage). He immediately informed the clerk that he did *not* intend to enroll in Medicare Part A. The clerk seemed surprised that he would want to reject it. In the end, she asked John four times, "Are you sure you don't want to sign up for Medicare?" All told, John assured the clerk four times that he did not want to sign up for Medicare. He completed the application by drawing a line through the statement that would have him applying for Medicare Part A, initialing the strikeout of the offending statement, and signing the altered application form.

Finally, John asked the clerk for a copy of the signed application, which showed he had struck out and initialed the statement that he was applying for Medicare Part A. The clerk, with some hesitation, gave him a copy. He returned home assuming he was not going to be enrolled in Medicare Part A without his written, informed consent.

Some five weeks later, John was surprised when he received a Medicare card in the mail. The card stated, "This is your Medicare card. It shows if you have hospital insurance, medical insurance, or both. . . . Show your card when you receive health services."

John's card showed that he had Medicare Part A. How could the government enroll him in the Medicare Part A program when he had explicitly declined enrollment? John later discovered that enrollment in Medicare Part A is mandatory if you want to receive Social Security benefits.

"I felt deceived," says John. "No one ever told me I would be forced to accept enrollment in Medicare in order to receive my Social Security retirement benefits." Like most Americans, John knew he was paying taxes to support the program. But he didn't know he would be forced to participate in Medicare Part A—the largest part of the Medicare program.

One might wonder why senior citizens, such as John, would want to reject "free" hospital insurance under Medicare Part A, especially since they've contributed payroll taxes to support the program for many years. Just as many parents forgo public education and instead choose to pay for private schooling (even though they've paid taxes and the public education is "freely" available to their children), seniors might choose to pay privately for their health insurance for a number of reasons. Consider, for example, that enrollment in Medicare automatically results in the following:

- The federal government dictates what types of services and treatments, including new life-saving technology, are "medically necessary" for seniors and what will be covered under Medicare.
- Medicare has the final say on hospital and doctor fees, and it requires providers to submit claims to the federal government. Those policies interfere with the doctor-patient relationship.
- Once enrolled in Medicare Part A (which happens automatically when one applies for Social Security benefits), the only way seniors can end their enrollment is by withdrawing from Social Security and repaying all cash benefits already paid to them.[3]
- The federal government effectively prohibits Medicare beneficiaries from paying privately for Medicare-covered services (most services).[4] The only way physicians can accept private payment from Medicare beneficiaries (for Medicare-covered services) is if they do not accept Medicare reimbursement (for treating Medicare patients) for two years. Since few doctors have enough Medicare patients who are willing to pay *all* their medical bills without Medicare reimbursement, the federal government realistically prevents seniors from spending their own money on the health care of their choice.[5] Yet, those under age 65 with employer-sponsored health insurance are free to pay privately (instead of having their insurers pay) for any medical care they choose.

These are just a few of the reasons seniors might choose to reject their entitlement to Medicare and instead pay privately for health insurance upon turning age 65.

These and many other startling facts about Medicare are not widely known among the general public. Here are some frequently asked questions about Medicare.

What Is Medicare?

Medicare is the largest single payer for health care in the United States, representing 12 percent of federal spending.[6] In 2000, it covered 39 million seniors and persons under 65 with certain disabilities.[7] Total program costs amounted to $221.8 billion in 2000

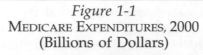

Figure 1-1
MEDICARE EXPENDITURES, 2000
(Billions of Dollars)

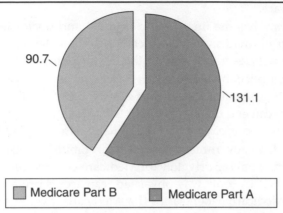

90.7

131.1

■ Medicare Part B   ■ Medicare Part A

SOURCES: Board of Trustees, Federal Hospital Insurance Trust Fund, *2001 Annual Report of the Board of Trustees of the Federal Hospital Insurance Trust Fund*, March 19, 2001. Board of Trustees, Federal Supplementary Medical Insurance Trust Fund, *2001 Annual Report of the Board of Trustees of the Federal Supplementary Medical Insurance Trust Fund*, March 19, 2001.

(Figure 1-1) and are projected to more than double over the next decade—reaching $491 billion by 2011.[8]

Medicare is administered by the Health Care Financing Administration (HCFA), recently renamed the Centers for Medicare and Medicaid Services (CMS) but hereafter referred to as HCFA, which contracts with insurance companies to process claims and pay medical bills. It is often confused with Medicaid, which is a government program for low-income children and adults. Both programs are administered by HCFA. But the major differences are that Medicare covers seniors and disabled persons regardless of their income, while Medicaid covers children, adults, and seniors who fall below a certain poverty level. Many seniors qualify for both Medicare and Medicaid—referred to as "dual eligibility." Approximately 6 million persons are dually eligible for both Medicare and Medicaid.[9] Together, Medicare and Medicaid represent the largest payer of health care in the world.[10]

When people hear the term Medicare, the first thing they should do is stop and ask, "Which part are you referring to?" There are big differences between the various parts of the program.

What Does Medicare Cover and How Is It Financed?

Medicare is primarily divided into two major parts. Part A (Hospital Insurance or HI) covers limited amounts of inpatient hospital care, home care, hospice care, and care in a skilled nursing facility.[11] Seniors are required to pay a deductible for each hospitalization (see Appendix A). This part of the program is financed by a 2.9 percent compulsory payroll tax.[12] Workers and employers each contribute 1.45 percent of workers' earnings. However, in reality the workers bear the full burden, because they ultimately receive lower wages when overall payroll taxes absorb a greater portion of their employers' total labor costs.

Taxes for Medicare Part A appear on each worker's earnings statement (W-2). That money, however, is not set aside for each worker's own future health care costs. Rather, today's Medicare payroll taxes are used for today's beneficiaries. In 2000, workers paid over $144 billion into the Medicare Part A trust fund.[13]

Part B (Supplementary Medical Insurance or SMI) pays for 80 percent (after seniors pay a $100 annual deductible) of approved doctor visits and other services not covered under Part A, such as ambulance services, outpatient hospital care, and X-rays (see Appendix B). It also covers some home care services and supplies. The majority of Part B spending—about 73 percent—is financed through general tax revenues. Another 23 percent comes from premiums paid by seniors, and the remaining 4 percent is financed by interest and other miscellaneous income. In 2000, taxpayers financed more than $65.9 billion toward doctor visits and outpatient medical services under Part B, and seniors contributed another $20.6 billion toward that part of Medicare.[14]

In addition, a Medicare Part C program, called Medicare + Choice, was established under the Balanced Budget Act of 1997. It was created to provide more choices and encourage seniors to enroll in private plans. Medicare beneficiaries were supposed to be offered choices among the following types of health plans: traditional fee-for-service (FFS) Medicare, health maintenance organizations

5

(HMOs), medical savings accounts (MSAs), preferred provider organizations (PPOs), or newly created provider sponsored organizations (PSOs).[15] The Congressional Budget Office (CBO) estimated that the Medicare Part C program would lead to significant enrollments in private plans. It estimated that enrollment would grow from 14 percent of all Medicare beneficiaries in 1997 to 25 percent by 2002.

However, according to Robert Waller, M.D., chairman of the Healthcare Leadership Council, burdensome government regulations encouraged private companies to withdraw from the Medicare-+Choice program. In February 2000, Dr. Waller told the Senate Finance Committee, "At first it seemed that plans were very willing to give Medicare+Choice a try. Forty new plans signed up in the first year following passage. But plans began withdrawing once they had begun to decipher the massive Medicare+Choice regulation published in 1998. . . . Now only 262 plans are signed up with Medicare+Choice, down from a high of 346 at the end of 1998."[16] As of January 2001, 14 percent of beneficiaries were enrolled in Medicare-+Choice programs and only 174 plans were participating in Medicare—approximately half the number participating in 1998 (Figure 1-2).[17]

Moreover, while appearing to give seniors unbiased choices, Medicare+Choice severely restricts the MSA option. That is because the new program limited the number of beneficiaries who can choose MSAs to only 390,000 out of 39 million enrollees.[18] Thus, only 1 percent of enrollees can choose an MSA, whereas all seniors can choose a managed care plan when it is available in their region.[19] No medical savings account plans have been approved for seniors. HCFA has entered into only one contract for a PSO, and only one private fee-for-service plan has been approved.[20] "While the aim of Medicare+Choice (M+C) was to expand choice, the choices available to Medicare beneficiaries have diminished since its inception," notes Marcia Gold, senior fellow at Mathematica Policy Research.[21]

The Part C program clearly maintains the government's position as purchaser and contractor of seniors' medical care. HCFA—not seniors—is the party who signs contracts with health plans and providers under all parts of Medicare (Parts A, B, and C). (See Table 1-1 for a comparison of Medicare Parts A and B and Medicaid.) In reality, the only plans seniors can choose from under the Medicare program are the ones HCFA decides to contract with and, conversely,

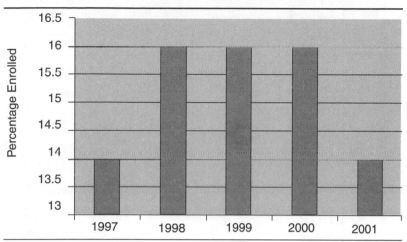

Figure 1-2
ENROLLMENT IN MEDICARE + CHOICE HMOS AND OTHER PLANS,
1997–2001

NOTE: All data are as of December of the given year. 2001 data are for January. HCFA/Center for Health Plans and Providers, 2000; Henry J. Kaiser Family Foundation, "Medicare Managed Care," *The Medicare Program,* February 2001.

those plans that agree to do business with the federal government. So the name "Medicare + Choice" is just that, only a name. It does not offer individuals true freedom of choice.

Does Medicare Provide Catastrophic Coverage?

As a citizen taxed to support the nearly $222-billion-a-year Medicare program, you probably assume that once you reach 65, it will provide you catastrophic coverage. It doesn't. Medicare doesn't pay for hospitalizations beyond 150 days, even though such hospitalizations would be considered truly catastrophic.[22] There is no cap on the amount of out-of-pocket costs that beneficiaries must pay. Medicare currently requires seniors to pay $792 for the first 60 days of each hospitalization, $198 per day for days 61–90, and $396 per day for days 91–150.[23] This is the opposite of sound insurance principles. Medicare should pay more—not less—when seniors face catastrophic illnesses. Because Medicare's hospital coverage is limited,

Table 1-1
MEDICARE AND MEDICAID: A COMPARISON

	Medicare Part A (Hospital Program)	Medicare Part B (Physician Services)	Medicaid (SCHIP & State-Based Programs)
Who is covered?	Seniors and certain disabled persons	Seniors and certain disabled persons	Low-income children, adults, seniors (including Medicare beneficiaries), and disabled persons
How is it financed?	Payroll taxes (employer and employee each pay 1.45%)	General taxes and seniors' premiums	Federal and state taxes
Is enrollment compulsory or voluntary?	Compulsory for most seniors*	Voluntary, but there are no other options for comprehensive coverage	Voluntary
Total costs: 2000	$131.1 billion	$90.7 billion	$116.4 billion (federal share) and $85.4 billion (state and local shares)**
Total persons enrolled: 2000	39 million	38 million	41.4 million (including 3.9 million seniors)***

* Medicare automatically enrolls most seniors in Medicare Part A when they turn 65. The only way seniors can forgo joining Part A is if they forgo their Social Security benefits. Because most seniors cannot afford that option, it is fair to say that Medicare Part A is essentially compulsory.
** Projected spending in 2000.
*** 1998 (most recently available figures).

SOURCES: HCFA, *A Profile of Medicaid: Chartbook 2000* (Washington: HCFA, September 2000); Board of Trustees, Federal Hospital Insurance Trust Fund, *2001 Annual Report of the Board of Trustees of the Federal Hospital Insurance Trust Fund*, March 19, 2001; Board of Trustees, Federal Supplementary Medical Insurance Trust Fund, *2001 Annual Report of the Board of Trustees of the Federal Supplementary Medical Insurance Trust Fund*, March 19, 2001; Stephen Heffler et al., "Health Spending Growth Up in 1999; Faster Growth Expected in the Future," *Health Affairs* 20, no. 2 (March/April 2001).

many seniors buy "Medigap" insurance to make sure they don't get stuck with huge medical bills.[24]

Medicare also generally doesn't cover long-term care expenses, such as nursing home care, unless seniors have been hospitalized.[25] For example, seniors cannot use the money they have contributed toward Medicare to pay for a nurse's aide to assist with bathing unless the service is connected to a hospitalization.

From its inception Medicare did not—and still does not—pay for many types of routine services. For example, it doesn't cover dental care, routine eye examinations, most prescription drugs, most nursing home care, and routine physical examinations. Medicare also doesn't cover many types of alternative medicine that are in great demand today, including acupuncture, homeopathy, and naturopathy. It covers only a limited amount of chiropractic care. (Appendices A, B, and C list covered and noncovered services.)

Do Taxpayers Have a Right to Their Medicare Contributions?

Most people assume that citizens are paying into the Medicare program and that the federal government will repay them benefits at some future date. However, it is important to stress that taxpayers don't have a binding contract with the U.S. government for future Medicare benefits.

The program was enacted as part of the Social Security Act Amendments of 1965, and the U.S. Supreme Court has ruled that Social Security is *not* a contributory insurance system because Social Security taxes are paid into the general treasury.[26] The trust fund is merely an accounting mechanism.

Individuals do not have a legally binding contractual right to their Social Security benefits.[27] The same is true for Medicare. It is a pay-as-you-go transfer program whereby the government collects money from today's taxpayers and uses it to pay part of today's seniors' medical bills. Congress and the President can change, add, or eliminate Medicare benefits at any time.

Does Medicare Pay Cash or Medical Benefits?

Medicare differs from the true insurance model in that it doesn't pay a lump-sum amount of cash to the insured individual, as a traditional indemnity plan does. Rather, it will provide reimbursement only for approved medical services. The difference is that indemnity insurance gives cash directly to patients and allows them to allocate the resources, whereas Medicare most often caps the amount providers can charge seniors for medical services.

Moreover, in most cases Medicare provides reimbursement to providers rather than seniors, thereby reducing seniors' incentive to become cost-conscious consumers.[28] Today's private medical insurance operates the same way, primarily because the government has manipulated the insurance market and has pushed insurance companies into following the model of the Blue Cross and Blue Shield plans, known as the "Blues."

Since the 1930s, the government has granted regulatory and tax advantages to Blue Cross plans, for hospital-based treatment, and Blue Shield plans, for physicians' treatment. These plans, which offer medical benefits instead of cash, have historically been run by physicians and hospitals and continue to receive the following regulatory advantages:

- Exemption from the general insurance laws of the state,
- Status as a charitable and benevolent organization,
- Exemption from the obligation of maintaining the reserves required of commercial insurers, and
- Tax exemption.[29]

In his book *Not What the Doctor Ordered*, Jeffrey Bauer explains how the Blues evolved to dominate the health insurance market. He explains that between the 1920s and 1960s, "organized medicine worked the legislatures to secure special treatment for its insurance plan—nonprofit status and exemption from insurance laws that required control by outside directors. With special treatment like this, the physician-controlled 'Blues' were able to corner the market on health insurance, too."[30] They were also successful in securing a large role in administering the Medicare program, while at the same time they were able to drop high-risk seniors from their health insurance risk pools. Today, Blue Cross and Blue Shield plans process approximately 90 percent of Medicare Part A claims and about 57 percent of all Part B claims.[31]

Is Medicare Compulsory or Voluntary?

The federal government automatically enrolls most seniors in Medicare Part A when they turn 65.[32] As John Pearson recently discovered, citizens cannot reject the hospital coverage (Part A) unless they *forgo all of the Social Security benefits they were taxed for and promised all their working lives.*[33] For many Americans, that option is too costly. Thus, many really don't have any other choice but to participate in Part A of Medicare.

When seniors are enrolled in Medicare Part A, the federal government also automatically enrolls them in Part B. They have the option of waiving entitlement in Part B without loss of Social Security benefits. But if seniors delay enrollment for more than a year from the time they are eligible for Part B, the premium cost goes up 10 percent and every additional year adds another 10 percent to their premium cost.[34] The penalty is applied during the entire time seniors are enrolled in Part B.[35]

That means, for example, if a senior waited three years to enroll, from the time he was eligible for Part B, he would have to pay 30 percent higher premiums for the entire time he was enrolled in Part B. What's more, although Medicare Part B is considered voluntary, seniors don't really have any other option but to join the program. That's because after Medicare was created in 1965, insurance companies canceled policies for seniors and encouraged them to enroll in Medicare.[36]

Today, there are no health insurance companies that will sell comprehensive health insurance to *Medicare-eligible seniors.* J. Patrick Rooney, Chairman of the Board Emeritus of Golden Rule Insurance Company, filed an affidavit in 1997 affirming that, to the best of his knowledge, there is no health insurance product available in the marketplace to U.S. citizens who are 65 years of age or older that would provide coverage in lieu of Medicare.[37] As discussed previously, there are a number of health plans that contract with Medicare under the Medicare + Choice program to provide health benefits to seniors. But those plans contract with the federal government, not directly with seniors, and they are required to follow an extensive set of federal rules.

Many seniors can purchase supplemental insurance (as opposed to comprehensive insurance) to pay for services *not* covered by Medicare. But most won't be able to opt out of Medicare Part B, because nothing exists in the marketplace that would provide coverage in place of Medicare.

When politicians decided in 1965 to make Medicare Part A compulsory and Medicare Part B nearly universal as well, they established a national policy to crowd out private insurance from the health care market for seniors.

The Outlook for Medicare: A Midlife Crisis

For years, health policy experts have been warning about the financial crisis looming in the future for Medicare. Each year, however, Congress continues to find funds to continue the program. That policymaking has worked for the most part because the number of seniors enrolling in the program has increased at a relatively steady rate.

During the past few years, Medicare growth has slowed compared to previous decades. In March 2001, the CBO projected that, for the period from fiscal year 1998 through fiscal year 2001, expenditures would increase at an average annual rate of 3.4 percent, compared with 10.0 percent during the previous decade.[38]

However, that slower growth rate will not be sustainable over the long run. In fact, the Treasury Department's June 2001 monthly statement of federal receipts and outlays revealed that Medicare spending is increasing rapidly again, rising 7.6 percent in the first eight months of fiscal year 2001, compared with the previous year.[39] The fundamental, long-term demographic factors likely to drive future Medicare spending much higher remain powerful and inescapable. The number of Medicare enrollees is projected to increase dramatically in 2011, when some 76 million baby boomers, born between 1946 and 1964, will start entering the program.[40] By 2020 the United States will have as many 65-year-olds as kindergartners.[41]

Other factors will also lead to overall Medicare growth in future years, including increases in per-beneficiary costs and longer time periods that beneficiaries will remain in Medicare. In December 2000, a new technical review panel advising Medicare trustees proposed more realistic assumptions for calculating long-term Medicare projections. The technical panel recommended assuming that future per-beneficiary costs for Medicare Part A and Part B combined eventually will grow at a rate of one percentage point above per capita growth in gross domestic product.[42] This revised growth rate—which was adopted in the 2001 Medicare trustees reports—is about one percentage point higher than previously assumed. Consequently, the estimated net present value of future additional resources needed to fund Part A benefits over the next 75 years increased from $2.6 trillion last year to $4.6 trillion in 2001—an increase of more than 75 percent.[43] The General Accounting Office (GAO) recently noted that the technical panel's new assumptions clearly demonstrate the significant implications of a one-percentage-point increase in annual Medicare spending over time.[44]

Annual Medicare expenditures are projected to more than double over the next decade, rising on average 7.7 percent per year.[45] At the same time, there will be fewer workers to pay for the promised benefits. So tomorrow's seniors will likely face higher out-of-pocket health care costs and more restricted choices than today's seniors.

The 2001 Medicare trustees annual report to Congress projects that under intermediate assumptions, the Part A trust fund will be completely depleted in 2029. That is an improvement over last year's estimate of 2025. Several factors account for the rosier picture: overall economic and job growth have provided a wider tax base to support the Medicare program, and there have been significant efforts to crack down on Medicare fraud and abuse.

Another important factor involved shifting two-thirds of Medicare home care expenditures—which had been the fastest-growing part of the program—from the hospital trust fund, financed by Medicare Part A payroll taxes, to the Part B trust fund for outpatient care, financed primarily by federal income taxes.[46] However, that led to increased spending on Medicare Part B. Medicare Part B expenditures now are projected to grow at a faster rate than Part A expenditures, and they could eventually surpass those of Part A spending totals (Figure 1-3).

President George W. Bush's budget plan recently noted how shifting home care costs to Part B was essentially an accounting gimmick:

> The previous Administration and Congress—in a transparent effort to further improve HI [Medicare Part A] solvency—also shifted a large portion of home health spending out of the HI trust fund to the SMI trust fund. This shift had no economic consequence, nor did it change total Medicare spending. But it did have the intended effect of making the HI trust fund appear more "solvent." Approximately one-third of the projected HI "surplus" over the next 10 years is due to this gimmick.[47]

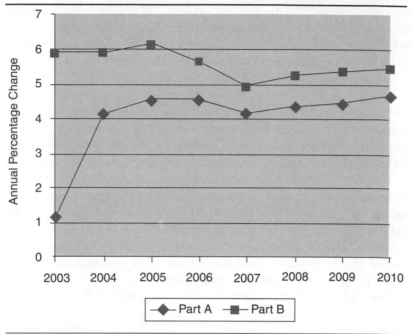

Figure 1-3

ESTIMATED ANNUAL PERCENTAGE CHANGE IN PER-BENEFICIARY
COSTS FOR MEDICARE PART A AND PART B, 2003–2010

SOURCE: Board of Trustees, Federal Hospital Insurance Trust Fund, *2001 Annual Report of the Board of Trustees of the Federal Hospital Insurance Trust Fund*, March 19, 2001, p. 92.

This sort of cost shifting, however, cannot continue indefinitely without seriously draining the national budget. In fact, Federal Reserve chairman Alan Greenspan projects that government programs to support a rapidly expanding aging population could threaten our nation's budget balance in the early decades of the 21st century. In 1998, he warned the National Bipartisan Commission on the Future of Medicare that our country's economic performance could be seriously jeopardized if preemptive action is not taken.[48] Leading financial experts warn that if the United States is going to maintain a balanced budget in the coming years, Medicare will need a major overhaul.

Nearly everyone agrees that Medicare's long-term projections pose significant concern. The 2001 Medicare trustees annual report to Congress notes that while the program's short-term insolvency date has improved, the long-range actuarial deficit is larger than previously projected. The CBO recently pointed out that although the outlook for the overall federal budget over the next decade is bright, long-term financing of Medicare continues to pose serious concerns. In January 2001, the CBO noted that over the longer term, "budgetary pressures linked to the aging and retirement of the baby-boom generation threaten to produce record deficits and unsustainable levels of federal debt."[49] Moreover, although the Medicare Part A trust fund is considered solvent until 2029 (under intermediate assumptions), that part of the Medicare program will begin running annual operating deficits after 2015, when its tax revenue falls short of expenditures. Thereafter, payroll tax funding falls short of Part A spending by widening amounts each year, until the entire trust fund is exhausted in 2029.[50]

Medicare's Impact on How Future General Revenue Will Be Spent

President Bush's 10-year budget plan (FY 2002–11) estimates a $645 billion total Medicare "deficit" between 2002 and 2011 (See Table 1-2). This figure includes spending for both Medicare Part A and Part B. Until recently, Medicare spending projections did not routinely combine both parts of Medicare. Today, however, budget experts stress the importance of examining both parts of the Medicare program in projecting expenditures. The GAO recently noted, "Measurement of Medicare's sustainability can no longer be merely the traditional measure of HI [hospital insurance] Trust Fund solvency that has been used to assess the program's financial status. Both Part A expenditures financed through its Trust Fund and Part B Supplementary Medical Insurance (SMI) expenditures financed through general revenues and beneficiary premiums must be taken into consideration."[51] In the same testimony the GAO stressed that this total spending approach is a much more realistic way of looking at Medicare's sustainability, noting, "In contrast, the historical measure of HI trust fund solvency cannot tell us whether the program is sustainable over the long haul. Worse, it can serve to distort the timing, scope, and magnitude of our Medicare challenge."

Table 1-2
TOTAL MEDICARE DEFICIT, 2002–11
(Billions of Dollars)

	2002 Estimate	Total 2002–11
Hospital Insurance (HI)–Medicare Part A		
HI Income	$181	$2,410
HI Spending	147	1,884
HI "Surplus"	34	526
Supplementary Medical Insurance (SMI)–Medicare Part B		
SMI Premiums	26	376
SMI Spending	112	1,547
SMI Deficit	86	1,171
Total Medicare Deficit	**$52**	**$645**

SOURCE: *A Blueprint for New Beginnings: A Responsible Budget for America's Priorities* (Washington: Government Printing Office, 2001), pp. 13–14.

NOTE: The Bush budget plan notes, "On a strictly cash basis (excluding HI interest), Medicare spending would exceed taxes and premiums by $51 billion in 2000, $66 billion in 2001, and $894 billion over the period of 2002 to 2011."

In President Bush's budget plan, *A Blueprint for New Beginnings: A Responsible Budget for America's Priorities,* he highlights the degree to which taxpayers will have to subsidize the gap between Medicare spending and Medicare payroll tax revenue during the next decade:

> From the perspective of the overall Federal budget, the [Medicare Part B] program is running a large deficit. . . . The [Medicare Part B] deficit is projected to total $86 billion in 2002 and $1.171 trillion over the period 2002 to 2011. This deficit in [Medicare Part B], combined with the [Medicare Part A] "surpluses", reveals a Medicare shortfall of $52 billion in 2002 and $645 billion over the period 2002 and 2011.[52]

The CBO has also recently stressed the need to examine Medicare Part B's future expenditures in relation to overall Medicare spending. "Medicare will become more and more dependent on general revenues and, ultimately, will be unsustainable in its current form," notes CBO director Dan Crippen.[53] In addition to greater general

Figure 1-4
PROJECTED MEDICARE PART A COSTS AS A PERCENTAGE OF
TAXABLE EARNINGS, 2001–2075

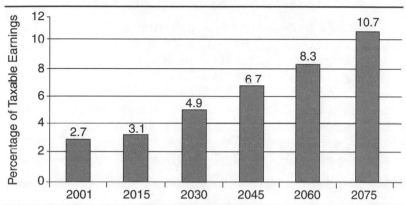

SOURCE: Board of Trustees, Federal Hospital Insurance Trust Fund, *2001 Annual Report of the Board of Trustees of the Federal Hospital Insurance Trust Fund*, March 19, 2001.

revenue expenditures for Part B, future taxpayers also face higher payroll taxes for Part A. The CBO points out that the number of beneficiaries in 2030 will be 90 percent greater than it is today, but the number of workers supporting Medicare will be only about 15 percent greater. Thus, Medicare Part A spending as a percentage of taxable payroll is expected to grow from 2.7 percent in 2000 to 4.9 percent in 2030 and to 10.7 percent by 2075 (Figure 1-4).[54]

Medicare has undoubtedly reached a midlife crisis and is going to require a major overhaul during the next decade. The fiscal squeeze on Medicare will be aggravated further by growing demands for more comprehensive medical services, including prescription drugs and preventive care. The program soon will not be able to pay all of its current promises, yet it faces mounting political pressure to take on new spending commitments. Box 1-1 provides a summary of the major problems facing the program, including financial and demographic factors.

Time for an Honest Debate

As we prepare for the upcoming Medicare debate, liberals will argue, as they have in the past, that Medicare is one of the greatest

---

Box 1-1
The Medicare Forecast: A Midlife Crisis

Medicare Is Projected to Go Bankrupt in 2029: The 2001 Medicare trustees report estimated that under intermediate economic projections, the Medicare hospital trust fund (Part A) would become insolvent in 2029. Under less favorable economic conditions (such as higher health care costs), it could become bankrupt as early as 2016.[55] Even under the intermediate economic assumptions, the Part A trust fund will begin running annual operating deficits after 2015. Annual Medicare Part A expenditures will increasingly outstrip the program's tax revenue, and the Part A trust fund will become bankrupt in 2029.

Medicare Part B is not projected for bankruptcy because it is heavily subsidized by general tax revenues. However, Part B continues to grow at a rate much faster than general inflation and continues to run large deficits.[56] In 2000, Part B expenditures increased 10 percent over the 1999 level.[57] The total Medicare deficit is estimated to be $645 billion over the period from FY2002 to FY2011.[58]

Baby Boomers Soon to Enter Medicare: Some 76 million baby boomers (born between 1946 and 1964) will start entering Medicare in the year 2011.[59] The total number of Medicare beneficiaries will grow from 39.6 million in 2000 to 69.3 million in 2025.[60]

Medicare Spending Rises: Annual Medicare expenditures are projected to climb from $238 billion to $679 billion (1998 inflation-adjusted dollars) between 2000 and 2025.[61] As a result, Medicare spending will become a much larger part of the federal budget. The GAO predicts that even without adding any new benefits, Medicare expenditures as a percentage of federal spending will rise from 12 percent currently to about 25 percent by mid-century.[62] Moreover, trends in Medicare Part B spending show no signs of slowing down. Higher rates are likely to continue in both the short-term and long-term outlook.

(continued next page)

(continued)

Fewer Workers per Retiree to Fund Medicare: As the number of persons entering Medicare rises sharply, there will be significantly fewer workers per retiree to pay for Medicare and other promised entitlements such as Social Security. By 2030, only 2.3 workers will be available to support each beneficiary compared to today's 4 workers per beneficiary.[63]

Beneficiaries' Out-of-Pocket Costs Rise: Medicare beneficiaries spend approximately 19 percent of their income on out-of-pocket health care costs.[64] That proportion is expected to rise to nearly 29 percent in 2025.[65] As Medicare costs rise over the years, the percentage that seniors must pay grows accordingly.

Reducing Waste, Fraud, and Abuse vs. Invading Privacy: Government officials estimate that Medicare fraud, abuse, and payment errors cost taxpayers $11.9 billion a year[66]—more than $32 million per day. Some health policy analysts point out that this figure may be high because inadvertent mistakes—such as improperly coding claims—are considered fraud.[67] Over the past few years, the federal government has increased its efforts to reduce Medicare fraud. Those efforts have undoubtedly increased medical privacy invasions. Washington attorney Jonathan Emord recently noted, "On the slightest suspicion of wrongdoing or billing impropriety, Medicare officials can order a doctor to turn over a Medicare patient's file." He also suggested that since recouped funds are deposited into a trust fund earmarked for Medicare-fraud enforcement, the fraud program creates a self-perpetuating prosecutorial machine. "With this vast expansion will come greater inquiry into patient files," warns Emord.[68]

governmental programs that ever existed in the United States and seniors now have access to medical care they couldn't get before the program was created.[69] But that claim is probably the greatest myth surrounding Medicare (see Box 1-2). Many people aren't aware of the fact that the United States already had a health care safety net in place for poor seniors before Medicare was created. In fact,

---

Box 1-2
The Greatest Medicare Myth

Myth: **Nearly half of all seniors did *not* have access to health care services prior to Medicare's enactment in 1965.**

Fact: This is probably the greatest myth surrounding Medicare. Today, many politicians cite a survey published in 1964 by the U.S. Department of Health, Education, and Welfare (HEW) claiming that only 54 percent of seniors had hospital insurance coverage. However, the survey is very misleading. It does not consider the fact that insurance does not equal access to health care. In fact, many persons had access to health care through other means. In particular, the HEW study specifically excluded persons (a) covered for accidental injury, a single disease or group of diseases, and loss of income (insurance that paid cash benefits instead of medical care); (b) covered under government health programs; (c) covered under welfare programs; and (d) covered as veterans and dependents of military personnel.[71]

Politicians who tout the 1964 HEW report conveniently overlook an important historical fact. Prior to the enactment of Medicare in 1965, there was already a government program to cover low-income seniors.[72] Nearly five years before Medicare was created, on September 13, 1960, President Dwight Eisenhower signed into law the "Medical Assistance for the Aged" program, commonly known as the Kerr-Mills law.[73] The program extended coverage to 10 million seniors whether or not they were receiving Social Security benefits and another 2.4 million on Old Age Assistance.[74]

All told, 77 percent of seniors (12.4 million out of 16 million) were eligible for government assistance under the Kerr-Mills program, according to the Senate Finance Report on the Social Security Amendments of 1960.[75] It was estimated that approximately one-half to one million seniors might become ill and require payments.[76]

(continued next page)

(continued)

The law established a new Title I of the Social Security Act, providing additional funds to the states to (a) establish a new, or improve their existing, medical care program for those on the old-age assistance rolls; and (b) add a new program designed to furnish medical assistance to those needy elderly citizens who were not eligible for old-age assistance but were financially unable to pay for medical and hospital care.

States were given flexibility in determining the standards for eligibility and scope of benefits to meet the health needs of the low-income aged in their respective states. However, states were required to provide benefits to seniors who reached age 65 and were not receiving old-age assistance, but whose income and resources were insufficient to meet the costs of necessary medical services. By 1964, the Kerr-Mills program was providing coverage to 475,000 seniors.

The Kerr-Mills program was similar to today's Medicaid program and the new State Children's Health Insurance Program (SCHIP). It was financed by both state and federal revenues. Seniors were subjected to a means test and had to prove a need before receiving benefits.

Supporters of national health care opposed the Kerr-Mills law because it was voluntary. They also argued that seniors were slow to enroll in the program. However, a 1960 survey conducted by researchers at Emory University found that nearly two-thirds of seniors reported they were in good health; only 10 percent reported being in poor health.[77] Today, 26.7 percent of seniors report being in fair or poor health.[78]

on September 13, 1960, President Dwight Eisenhower signed into law the Medical Assistance for the Aged (MAA) program, creating a health care "safety net" for 77 percent of seniors (12.4 million out of 16 million).[70] The program was means tested and was funded by both the federal government and state governments. It was similar to today's Medicaid program. Box 1-2 provides a more detailed description of the MAA program.

Many Democrats and Republicans alike were opposed to the compulsory Medicare program in the early 1960s. However, supporters of national health care consistently produced studies, public opinion polls, and testimony that eventually swayed the Democrats and nearly half of all Republicans in Congress to support the final Medicare bill in 1965. Since then, Medicare has become a third rail for most politicians, meaning "touch it and your political career will die." Consequently, today even Republicans vow to "protect and preserve" Medicare, with the misunderstanding that seniors wouldn't have access to health care without it.

Do policymakers and most Americans truly understand what is being protected and preserved under the Medicare program? Do they realize how the program came about, how it affects nearly every taxpayer and senior today, and how it will affect them tomorrow?

It is clear that Medicare is going to need to be re-examined and restructured in the near future. Nearly everyone will be affected by the changes ahead. Workers would likely be forced to pay higher taxes—both payroll taxes and general taxes—if the program isn't reformed on sound economic principles. At the same time, tomorrow's seniors could be forced to pay higher copayments, deductibles, and other out-of-pocket expenses for medical care. Providers and hospitals could face reduced payments, ultimately affecting the quality of medical care for seniors. Future beneficiaries are not going to settle for inadequate medical care during old age. Yet tomorrow's workers are going to be asked to pay an ever-growing percentage of payroll taxes to support future Medicare costs and benefits.

The road ahead is going to require some tough choices. Taxpayers and seniors need to become better informed about Medicare reform. They will have to decide whether they want to resolve the mounting Medicare tensions—higher costs and greater demands for coverage—in the marketplace or through the political process.

22

The first step to a fair and full debate about Medicare reform involves examining the program's history, evolution, and outcomes. Providing historical insights will help Americans make informed decisions about how Medicare should be reformed and whether private markets will play a greater role in delivering health care to seniors.

2. The Push for Compulsory Health Insurance: Early International and National Efforts

To understand how compulsory health insurance (Medicare) came about in the United States, it is important to first examine what was happening around the world and then consider how philosophical and economic factors in the United States fostered the development of compulsory health insurance as we know it today. An examination of these issues provides an overview of how U.S. policy follows international trends and how progressive politics and economic downturns have played a large role in shaping our system. This chapter also provides a significant discussion of the first national study of the U.S. health care system—a study that would shape the system for years to come.

International Trends

The movement toward compulsory health insurance began in the late 19th century in Germany, where, under the leadership of Chancellor Otto von Bismarck, the "social insurance" philosophy was introduced.[1] That philosophy held that the state has a right to regulate the interaction of classes and interests for the advancement of the general welfare, including health care.[2] Bismarck embraced a compulsory health care system financed by employee and employer contributions, in which the wealthy contributed more than the poor. Under Bismarck's leadership, the German Sickness Insurance Act was passed on June 16, 1883.[3]

Soon various forms of compulsory health coverage were established in other European countries: Austria (1888), Hungary (1891), Denmark (1892), Luxembourg (1901), Norway (1909), Serbia (1910), Great Britain (1911), Russia (1912), Romania (1912), and the Netherlands (1913).[4]

Peter Corning, a journalist commissioned by the Social Security Administration to write about the evolution of Medicare, notes that acceptance of social insurance by the British in 1911 had a profound effect on some American political and intellectual leaders. Britain, he explains, was at the height of her power and much admired and emulated in the United States. "A movement to enact social insurance (starting with health insurance) on a State-by-State basis began in this country almost immediately after the passage of the British National Health Insurance Program in 1911," reports Corning.[5] It wasn't until the 1960s, however, that the social insurance philosophy of health care was officially adopted in North America. The United States enacted compulsory hospital insurance for seniors (Medicare Part A) in 1965, and Canada established its medicare program, which mandated compulsory health insurance for all ages, in 1968.[6]

Politics and Early Efforts in the United States

In the United States, the call for national health insurance dates back to 1904 when the Socialist party first advocated it.[7] The Socialist party's official national platform called for "the insurance of the workers against accident, sickness and lack of employment" and for "pensions for aged and exhausted workers."[8] During that period, social activists and academicians began recommending government health care.

In 1906, academicians at the University of Wisconsin established the American Association for Labor Legislation (AALL) to study social insurance issues.[9] Despite its name, AALL did not formally represent organized labor. In fact, leaders of the American Federation of Labor (AFL) were initially opposed to government health insurance and did not officially endorse the principles of social insurance until some 26 years later.[10]

In 1912, the Progressive party and its presidential candidate, Theodore Roosevelt, espoused national health insurance as a campaign issue.[11] During that same year, the AALL set up a Committee on Social Insurance composed of political scientists, economists, trade unionists, and lawyers. The Committee set out to promote government health insurance by educating and influencing three primary groups: major private interest groups and associations, the lay public, and state legislators and governors. The Committee established study groups with private associations "in the hope that such groups would stimulate discussion and produce a favorable consensus within the organization[s] for public declaration of support." It also targeted the public through disseminating reports, communicating extensively with newspaper editors around the country, and encouraging national press coverage of health care issues.[12]

By 1915, AALL's Committee had released recommendations for compulsory health insurance and begun drafting model legislation at the state level.[13] Advocates tended to concentrate their efforts in the states until 1937, when the U.S. Supreme Court ruled in *Helvering v. Davis* that national social insurance was constitutional.[14] Prior to the 1930s, the U.S. Supreme Court and leading constitutional lawyers interpreted the Constitution in such a way that social welfare matters were under the jurisdiction of the states. The AALL's model legislation, however, did not include specific provisions regarding medical services. Those details would be left to organized medicine.

At that time, President Theodore Roosevelt's personal physician, Dr. Alexander Lambert, chaired an American Medical Association (AMA) committee on social insurance. That committee was created to provide the medical details for AALL's model bill.[15] Proceedings from the 67th annual session of the AMA in 1916 explain:

> The [AMA's House of Delegates] secretary received from Dr. John B. Andrews, secretary of the American Association for Labor Legislation, a pamphlet containing a tentative draft of a model bill for industrial insurance, together with an editorial for publication in *The Journal* and the *Press Bulletin*. In this tentative bill, the provisions regarding medical services were intentionally omitted in order that this entire question might be taken up by the representatives of the organized medical profession and properly discussed.[16]

After consulting with the medical profession, the AALL completed drafting its model legislation. By 1917, the AALL's proposed legislation for compulsory health insurance had been introduced in 12 state legislatures, including California, Massachusetts, and New Jersey.[17] Several prominent governors, including California's Hiram Johnson, strongly endorsed the legislation.[18] The momentum for social insurance, however, was stalled by World War I (1914–1918).[19]

Compulsory health insurance became negatively linked with "made in Germany" and "Bolshevism."[20] The links with Germany and Russia created a postwar reaction to progressivism that dampened enthusiasm for social insurance in the United States.[21] In fact, a California voter referendum on compulsory health insurance was defeated by a 2 to 1 margin in 1918. Soon after the California defeat the campaign for compulsory health insurance collapsed. Not a single state had enacted the model legislation, notes Corning.[22]

Organized medicine, too, experienced a change in the political tide following World War I. Richard Harris, a former reporter for *The New Yorker*, points out that when the United States entered the war, a great many doctors from around the country started writing letters to the *Journal of the American Medical Association* to express disapproval of the model state legislation.[23] This, in turn, prompted county and state medical societies to send AMA official resolutions condemning its position. "By 1920, the outcry against the model bill had become so clamorous that the AMA's House of Delegates reversed itself and passed a resolution declaring its 'opposition to the institution of any plan embodying the system of compulsory contributory insurance against illness,'" reports Harris.[24]

Economic Factors and the Manifesto for National Health Insurance

Despite widespread opposition to compulsory health insurance, a small group of national leaders, mostly medical doctors, persuaded eight philanthropic foundations to underwrite a commission to study the nation's health care system.[25] In 1927, the Committee on the Costs of Medical Care (CCMC) was created under the chairmanship of Dr. Ray Lyman Wilbur, a past president of the AMA, president of Stanford University, and soon to be secretary of the interior under President Herbert Hoover.[26] The CCMC—which consisted of prominent figures in medicine, public health, social work, education, and public affairs[27]—began its studies in 1927 when, according to Isadore Falk, CCMC's associate director of study, "our economy was climbing toward a high peak of prosperity." However, that economic outlook would soon change.

Charles-Edward A. Winslow served as chairman of the CCMC's executive committee and was most responsible for effecting the compromise embodied in the final recommendations.[28] In 1917 Winslow had visited Russia, whose health care system he admired. According to historian Arthur Viseltear, "Visiting Russia in 1917, Winslow had observed firsthand the great progress based on the

Russian administrative structure and on the 'remarkable development of social medicine along curative lines and the consequent
close connection between curative and preventive work.' It was this
tendency—to use the physician as a 'real force' in prevention by
organizing machinery for the medical examination of well persons
or of those in the early and incipient stages of disease—that he
hoped to see developed in the United States.''[29]

The CCMC completed its work by 1932, when the nation was
plunging toward economic depression. During the time the CCMC
was conducting its research and preparing reports, another significant change occurred: the first hospital insurance program was created in the United States at Baylor University Hospital in Dallas in
1929. That program was established to reduce the hospital's unpaid
patient care bills, according to Harvard medical economist Rashi
Fein. Initially it covered only Dallas schoolteachers. But Fein notes
how the program grew:

> It is not surprising that the Baylor plan, though offering
> limited benefits restricted to a single hospital, proved popu-
> lar. The schoolteachers enrolled and the prepayment method
> of financing was quickly introduced to other groups in Dal-
> las. Hospital administrators in other parts of the United
> States, facing similar problems, took note of what had tran-
> spired in Dallas. Prepayment, they concluded, might be the
> key to a hospital's financial stability.[30]

Meanwhile, the CCMC published some 26 reports over five years,
between 1928 and 1932.[31] It undertook the first comprehensive study
of the U.S. health care system, including physician and hospital
financing, public health services, and medical education and training. Its final report in 1932, *Medical Care for the American People*,
asserted that Americans were not seeking enough medical care. It
also reported an oversupply of medical specialists and nurses and
low occupancy rates for hospitals: some 25 to 40 percent of the
nation's civilian hospital beds were empty in 1931.[32] In addition, a
survey of 38,668 persons found that among the lowest income group,
46.6 percent received no medical care, compared to 13.8 percent in
the highest income group.[33] The CCMC interpreted those findings
to mean that the nation's health care costs needed to be redistributed
more evenly to improve access for all.

At the same time, the CCMC acknowledged that there had been great improvements in the nation's health over the previous 50 years. As Dr. Wilbur noted in the report's introduction (in 1932):

> Medical science has made marvelous advances during the last fifty years. Following the work of Pasteur, Lister and Koch remarkable progress has been made in controlling the communicable diseases, and the average length of life during this period has been greatly extended. . . . We have the knowledge, the techniques, the equipment, the institutions, and the trained personnel to make even greater advances during the next fifty years. . . . The report affords for the first time a scientific basis on which the people of every locality can attack the perplexing problem of providing adequate medical care for all persons at costs within their means.[34]

The CCMC further reported that new knowledge of nutrition was yielding remarkable results in the treatment and prevention of many deficiency diseases. It warned, however, that a vast amount of disease was still preventable and many thousands of persons were not receiving adequate treatment.[35]

All told, the CCMC recommended group *payment* for medical care through insurance, taxation, or both. It approved of insurance only insofar as it was controlled by the medical profession. The CCMC denounced private insurance companies, claiming, "The participation by commercial insurance companies in the forms of insurance against the costs of medical care which are recommended in this report would, the Committee believes, tend to increase the costs and not to improve the quality of service."[36]

The CCMC also recommended group medical practice over solo practice and the expansion of preventive and basic public health services for all. And it called for America to devote more resources to health care.[37] The final report states as follows:

> With growth of national income which is probable in the next two or three decades, far larger amounts will be spent advantageously and without hardship. An increased national income can be used in only three ways: to purchase more consumers' goods, to purchase more services, or to provide savings. Since the country is now suffering, in part, from an excess of savings in the form of capital goods, a large increase of productive facilities is not called for. While there is at present underconsumption of food, clothing, housing, and

> of commodities in general, the increase in the national income
> during the next ten or twenty years would yield the largest
> satisfactions if a large proportion of it were spent for services,
> especially for medical care, education, and cultural pursuits.[38]

In 1932, the nation was spending $3.2 billion a year on medical care, approximately $38.9 billion in 1999 dollars.[39] Health spending represented about 4 percent of total national spending compared to 13.5 percent today.[40] The report proposed that Americans who could not afford medical care should rely less on private charity and more on the taxpayers. The CCMC argued that the plan for "satisfactory" medical care could best be attained by a process of evolution. It recognized that it might take some 20 or 30 years of public education before its recommendations would be implemented.[41]

The CCMC was also concerned with the growing use of alternative medicine.[42] It suggested that there should be better control over the quality of medical care, noting that less than one-third of drugs and medicines were used "on the express order of physicians" and that patent medicines represented 10 percent of the total spent on medical services and commodities.[43] The report noted, "Practice by unqualified 'cult' practitioners should be eliminated, and control should be exercised over the practice of secondary practitioners, such as midwives, chiropodists, and optometrists."[44] It recommended licensing laws for drugs, state regulation of home care provided by nurses' aides, and state registration and physician supervision of midwives.[45]

In addition to the 150-page majority report, the CCMC published a 34-page minority report that differed in many respects.[46] The minority report supported a compulsory health plan under government and professional control.[47] It endorsed *group payment* for medical care but it condemned group practice and contract practice, noting, "The evils of contract practice are widespread and pernicious."[48] It argued that contracts should be considered unethical if they allow solicitation of patients or encourage competition and underbidding to secure a contract. Competitive bidding, the minority report argued, would lower the quality of medical care.[49]

The development of health plans under the auspices of state or county societies was recommended as an alternative to commercial insurance. The minority report provided eight guiding principles for financing medical care this way:

- Plans must be under control of the medical profession.
- Plans must guarantee free choice of physician.
- Plans must include nearly all members of the county medical society.
- Funds must be administered on a nonprofit basis.
- Patients should pay a certain minimum amount, with the common fund providing only the portion beyond the patient's means.
- Plans should make adequate provisions for community care of the indigent.
- Plans must be entirely separate from any plan providing for cash benefits.
- Plans must not require certification of disability by the physician treating the disease or injury.[50]

The work of the CCMC would influence health care in the United States for many years. The AMA later approved the minority report, according to Falk, who served as CCMC's associate director of study during the 1930s.[51]

The CCMC's final report became known as "the manifesto of liberal health reform in the United States," according to the *International Journal of Health Services*.[52] Furthermore, Falk later wrote "the [CCMC] Report nevertheless changed the course and, in some measure, the pace of evolution for the health services in the United States."[53] Falk explains that by 1932 the widespread economic depression precipitated a financial crisis for medical providers, compelling the prompt development of health insurance as recommended by the CCMC. Referring to the study's impact on establishing health insurance, Falk noted, "This was the beginning of massive growth of private insurance through what was to become the Blue Cross, the Blue Shield and the commercial insurance patterns." That change of course is evidenced by today's growth in prepaid health plans that provide medical benefits and a reduction in traditional indemnity policies and cash payments for health care.

One of the CCMC's most striking recommendations was for physicians to join group practices rather than practice on their own. State medical societies and the AMA fought hard in the ensuing years to oppose that recommendation. In fact, in 1938 the AMA and the District of Columbia Medical Society were indicted for violating the

Sherman Antitrust Act's prohibition on restraint of trade. They were convicted of expelling or threatening to expel salaried group practice doctors from their societies and using coercive power to deprive them of hospital facilities for their patients. The Supreme Court upheld the convictions in 1943.[54] Justice Owen J. Roberts, writing for a unanimous court, said:

> Professions exist because people believe they will be better served by licensing specially prepared experts to minister to their needs. The licensed monopolies which professions enjoy constitute in themselves severe restraints upon competition. But they are restraints which depend upon capacity and training, not privilege. Neither do they justify concerted criminal action to prevent the people from developing new methods of serving their needs. The people give the privilege of professional monopoly and the people may take it away.[55]

After the ruling, the AMA continued to oppose prepaid group health insurance through less overt tactics, according to Harris.[56] Thereafter, the push for national health care was stymied temporarily by, of all things, a doctors' boycott of the Borden Company.

Albert G. Milbank was chairman of Borden and the Milbank Fund, an underwriter of the CCMC, and a strong supporter of national health care. Borden produced irradiated evaporated milk for infants. To get Milbank and his fund to back off national health insurance, several medical journals launched a subtle effort to have doctors boycott the milk. Eventually, the *Philadelphia Medical Roster & Digest* could report that "one of the foundations has already modified its elaborate plan to sell state medicine for the simple but effective reason that many discerning physicians had stopped buying a certain product."[57]

By 1929, health care spending amounted to $29.49 per capita (or 4.2 percent of per capita personal income), with the largest portion spent on visits to doctors, not hospital care, according to U.S. census data.[58] That amounts to approximately $287.31 per capita in 1999 dollars. Medical historian Paul Starr explains that physicians' prices were rising, thanks to the medical profession's increasing monopoly power, which resulted from licensing restrictions and other practices.[59]

What the CCMC Final Report Did *Not* Say

It is interesting to note that the CCMC's final report—the nation's first large study on medical costs—did not estimate the number of Americans lacking insurance. Perhaps one reason is that the push for compulsory health insurance had more to do with politics than insurance.

"The historical origins of health insurance as a public program," explains Starr, "are linked more to concerns about income maintenance, national economic power, and political stability than they are to the financing of medical care."[60] Another reason might be that organized medicine, whose former president chaired the CCMC, did not support the widespread use of commercial insurance that paid cash benefits.[61]

Susan Feigenbaum, associate professor of economics at the University of Missouri, explains that in the early 1900s mutual aid societies underwrote a large number of "sickness" insurance policies.[62] Sickness insurance differed from today's health insurance in that it provided cash payments—not medical services—to sick workers.

By 1932, there were more than 900 mutual benefit associations providing cash benefits and over 500 fraternal societies providing medical benefits during illness.[63] Trade unions and private companies also provided medical benefits to workers. In 1932, there were about 100 national or international trade unions providing medical benefits to members, and there were a few large industrial organizations that had staffs of salaried physicians, dentists, nurses, and laboratory workers who provided complete medical services for workers and their families. This arrangement concerned organized medicine because it used contracts and competitive bidding. Medical leaders argued that such arrangements would reduce the quality of medical care.[64]

In addition, by 1932 all but four states had adopted compulsory worker's compensation laws, providing benefits for accidents and occupational diseases.[65] Another type of coverage that was commonly sought among workers during the early 1900s was "industrial" insurance. Those policies provided lump-sum cash payments at death to pay for funerals and costs associated with terminal illnesses. A 1901 Bureau of Labor study of 2,567 families found that 65.8 percent had such policies.[66] Insurance premiums were commonly paid weekly. Starr notes, however, that workers received only about 40 cents of every dollar they paid in premiums.[67] The remainder was spent on administrative costs and company profits. Supporters of compulsory health insurance argued that the costs would be better spent on direct patient care.

The New Deal

Another important period in the evolution of compulsory health insurance was President Franklin D. Roosevelt's New Deal. During the Great Depression, many Americans could not pay for food and shelter, let alone medical services.[68] To mitigate the effects of the Depression, Roosevelt in mid-1934 established (through an executive order) a Committee on Economic Security to draft plans for a Social Security program. The Committee made recommendations for federal funding of pensions, unemployment insurance, and cash assistance for the poor. It also proposed "an official study be made of the practicability of national health insurance."[69]

The Social Security legislation that went to Congress in 1935 empowered the Social Security Board to study the idea of national health insurance. However, there was much opposition to the idea. Said the staff director of the Committee, "That little line [inserted into the Social Security bill] was responsible for so many telegrams to the members of Congress that the entire social-security program seemed endangered."[70]

The line was struck out to ensure passage of the Social Security Act (which became law in 1935). President Roosevelt pursued the issue no further because he feared it would ruin his chances for reelection.[71] Thus the push for national health care was put on hold for a short time.

When Americans were asked in 1946, "What do you think should be done, if anything, so that people can get the hospital and medical care they need and make it easier for them to pay these bills?", only 11 percent chose "Socialized medicine under head of [management of] Social Security." Only 1 percent were in favor of a national health program (today's Medicare program). Twenty-five percent supported the use of *voluntary* health insurance and prepaid care; 18 percent had no opinion, weren't sure, or didn't answer; and 9 percent said nothing should be done. The rest supported one of 13 other options, such as free clinics or private charity, with no more than 5 percent of respondents selecting any of these categories.[72]

Even so, from 1939 onward congressional bills proposing compulsory health insurance for the entire population were introduced each year.[73] There was an especially significant push for national health care in 1950, but no legislation passed.

The very breadth of the proposals—universal coverage—was the prime reason for their failure. However, after many trials and errors, proponents finally devised a strategy to narrow their scope, thus increasing the likelihood of success. By all accounts, two of the men most responsible for developing an incremental strategy were Wilbur Cohen and Isadore Falk. Both had been advisers to Oscar Ewing, head of the Federal Security Agency, the government organization in charge of setting up and administering Social Security.[74] Howard Berliner, an academician and supporter of national health care,[75] describes the incremental approach that proponents of compulsory health insurance resorted to:

> With the final defeat of compulsory national health insurance in 1950, the reformers looked for another means to accomplish their ends. Because they still wanted national health insurance, they adopted a strategy of incrementalism or, as it was more commonly referred to, "getting a foot in the door." The idea was to bring about the passage of a modest program of insurance for a small number of people, and then gradually to expand that program until it covered the entire population. The question then arose of which group would be insured first. It was at this point that the movement in the United States toward national health insurance diverged from the international trend [of usually starting with industrial workers and their families]. Many of the country's health reformers at that time were working for the federal government in the Social Security Administration. These reformers, having had working experience with the health problems and needs of the aged, opted to make the elderly the initial group to be insured.[76]

Truman Introduces the Incremental Strategy

President Harry Truman was probably most responsible for putting the incremental strategy for national health care into action. He had been a strong supporter of the idea and made it part of his 1948 presidential campaign. This gained him the support of organized labor (whose leadership had changed over the years in favor of compulsory health insurance) and the opposition of organized medicine.[77] At first he proposed a large-scale plan, but when it got nowhere in the late 1940s, he resorted to the incremental approach.

In 1951, Truman set up the Commission on the Health Needs of the Nation, composed of leaders in medicine, labor, public health, and education. The members were instructed to study the nation's health care system and report their findings within a year.[78] The chairman of the Commission was Dr. Paul B. Magnuson, a noted surgeon, a Republican, and an outspoken opponent of national health insurance. Ironically, he would help devise the strategy that eventually created the Medicare program.

The Commission held extensive hearings around the country and in 1952 submitted a report titled "Building Americans' Health." The report emphasized Cohen and Falk's incremental approach. Instead of focusing on the entire population, as Democrats had been doing over the years, the Commission proposed a much narrower program: prepaid health benefits for people on Social Security—that is, the elderly, the widowed, and the disabled.

Truman's Commission began comparing the health statistics of the aged with those of younger populations. The profiles supported the popular conception that seniors were sicker, poorer, and less insured than younger Americans.[79] According to Yale professor Theodore Marmor, "The concentration on the burdens of the aged was a ploy for sympathy."[80] Armed with new statistics, the proponents could more effectively promote their agenda. Consequently, "a new series of health insurance bills . . . became the focus of legislative issues for the years 1952–1965," reports Falk.[81] While a federal compulsory health insurance program was not adopted until 1965, a program for low-income seniors was created in 1960 that provided subsidies for many, as discussed in the following chapter.

In summary, early efforts to institute compulsory health insurance in the United States were fostered by several factors, including (a) the growing acceptance of compulsory health programs among other industrialized nations, (b) poor economic conditions during the Depression, and (c) large national studies sponsored by prominent foundations and organizations. In particular, the CCMC's 1932 report *Medical Care for the American People* laid the foundation for shaping U.S. health policy for years to come. History shows us that scholarly research and analyses can have a great impact on directing health policy decisions. The use of health statistics was very important in shaping the public's opinion about the uninsured elderly and in eventually bringing us a national compulsory health insurance program.

3. Medicare's Enactment in the United States: From State to Federal Coverage

Although large-scale efforts to create a national health care system in the United States failed during the early and mid-1900s, the incremental approach adopted in the 1950s would soon prove to be effective. An examination of how compulsory health insurance in the United States began with federally subsidized state programs and then shifted to the federal level provides an important history lesson. In the end, the final passage of Medicare took a lot of political manipulation and deal making. This chapter examines that process.

State Health Coverage for Seniors

One of the biggest myths surrounding Medicare is that it was enacted because seniors had no means to pay for medical care in the 1960s. In fact, in 1960 (five years before Medicare was enacted), Congress passed a law to provide federal funds to states to cover the medical needs of low-income seniors.[1] The law was commonly known as the "Kerr-Mills program," named after sponsors Sen. Robert Kerr (D-Okla.) and Rep. Wilbur Mills (D-Ark.). It was also referred to as the Medical Assistance for the Aged (MAA) program. The Kerr-Mills program was much more generous than Medicare because in many states it covered dental services and prescription drugs.[2] To qualify, seniors had to undergo means testing to prove their financial need.

The Kerr-Mills/MAA program had tremendous bipartisan support in the 86th Congress in 1960. Mills, chairman of the powerful Ways and Means Committee, was a strong proponent and cosponsor. President Eisenhower supported the measure because it was voluntary in nature. He was adamantly opposed to Sen. John F. Kennedy's alternative proposal for a compulsory health insurance program under Social Security. As the *Wall Street Journal* reported, "The Eisenhower Administration privately has accepted the Kerr proposal on the ground it doesn't damage Mr. Eisenhower's demand that any medical care plan avoid the 'compulsory' Social Security approach."[3] Many Democrats were also opposed to the Kennedy approach.

In August 1960, the Democratic-controlled Senate Finance Committee voted down the Kennedy proposal 12 to 5 while approving the Kerr-Mills bill by a 12-to-4 vote.[4] On August 23, 1960, the Senate rejected an amendment by Senator Kennedy (51 to 44) to finance medical care for the aged by an increase in Social Security taxes.[5] However, on that same day, the Senate passed the Kerr-Mills bill by a vote of 89 to 2.[6] On September 13, 1960, President Eisenhower signed the Kerr-Mills bill into law. It was officially titled the Social Security Amendments of 1960 (Public Law 86-778).[7]

The Kerr-Mills program went into effect October 1, 1960. Its success would depend on whether the federal government could administer it effectively and whether states chose to participate. One of those most responsible for instituting the program was Wilbur Cohen, a devoted supporter of government health care.

In 1961, when the federal government began implementing the Kerr-Mills program, Cohen held the important position of assistant secretary for legislation at the U.S. Department of Health, Education, and Welfare (HEW).[8] He later wrote, "Although I had been a strong advocate of a comprehensive and universal nationwide health insurance plan since 1940, I was conscious of the monumental administrative and management problems involved in such a large undertaking. My professors and mentors had stressed administrative competence in social legislation. The merits of the incremental approach ... [were] always in the forefront of my mind."[9]

By the end of August 1961, legislation establishing state programs had been passed or was in the process of being enacted in 33 states. A 1961 HEW annual report to Congress concluded:

> The content of medical care service for which costs are assumed for recipients of old-age assistance [Social Security] is considered comprehensive or relatively so in 26 States. These States provide for hospitalization, nursing home care, and physicians' services without significant limitations as to the nature of the patient's illness, unit cost of care, number of days of care, or number of visits to or from a doctor. While several of these States have some limitations, most of them meet the cost of practically any needed and available care.[10]

40

By November 30, 1964, 39 states and the District of Columbia had established programs providing medical assistance for the aged. All covered hospital services; 30 covered nursing home care; 34 covered doctor visits; and 25 covered prescription drugs.[11] However, some states limited the amount of covered services, like today's Medicare. The programs also required seniors to undergo a means test to qualify.

Proponents of government-controlled medical care strongly opposed the means testing requirement, arguing that health care is a "right" for all. Moreover, they complained that states were slow to use the federal funds. Some suggested that the government's tardiness was no accident and that the program was designed to fail, thus paving the way for a full national health care program.

The suspicion that HEW was sabotaging Kerr-Mills came to the forefront in 1965 when Sen. John Williams (R-Del.) questioned Dr. Donovan Ward, president of the AMA, during a Senate Finance Committee hearing. Following is their exchange:

> Senator Williams: Is not also one of the major reasons that the Kerr-Mills bill was not implemented more rapidly by the respective States that since its enactment in 1960 the Department [HEW] here in Washington has been discouraging the States and propagandizing against the Kerr-Mills bill trying to keep it from enacting it in order that they might force the King-Anderson [Medicare] bill or some medical bill of its comparison into law?

> Dr. Ward: We believe this is true, sir.

> Senator Williams: I know in our own state representatives of the department have spoken against it and even to the extent that last year there was such a confusion created that the Governor of the State thought the Kerr-Mills bill had been implemented when it is not implemented in reality and the first payments are going out in 1965.

> Dr. Ward: Yes, sir; we believe had the Secretary of HEW given support for the Kerr-Mills bill, it would have been implemented more rapidly in all of the states.[12]

HEW might have stalled the program because it was voluntary and required means testing, which was contrary to universal coverage. Proponents of universal coverage wanted a compulsory program for seniors of all incomes, financed by Social Security taxes.

41

Was There Really a Crisis of Uninsured Seniors?

During the 1960s, advocates of government action pointed out that rates of hospitalization were greatest among seniors and that nearly half of the elderly didn't have health insurance.[13] Among other objectives, proponents claimed that a new Medicare program would reduce the amount of money seniors paid out of pocket for health care. What most people don't realize is that seniors were increasingly gaining access to health care and health insurance.

In the 10 years before Medicare's enactment, the number of retirees with health insurance nearly doubled. According to testimony by the health insurance industry during a 1965 congressional hearing on Medicare, "In 1952, there were 31 percent of that age group [65- to 74-year-olds] with [health insurance] coverage, in 1956 there was 44 percent, a 13 percent increase or more than a third; in 1959, 53 percent," noted H. Lewis Rietz, testifying on behalf of American Life Convention, Health Insurance Association of America and Life Insurers Council.[14] Rietz also pointed out, "In July 1961 we estimated that 53 percent of the non-institutionalized aged population were covered by some form of voluntary health insurance. Continuing dynamic growth has resulted in a significantly increased proportion of the aged having coverage today. By 1962, 60 percent of the aged [65 and over] had voluntary health insurance." Coverage for the nonelderly was also on the rise during that period, indicating that the nation as a whole was moving toward greater health insurance coverage.

During the debate over Medicare, supporters argued that nearly half of all seniors had no health insurance. They often cited a 1964 HEW report showing that only 54 percent of the 17 million persons over 65 had hospitalization insurance versus 70.3 percent of the general population.[15] However, the HEW study excluded seniors who were covered under government health and welfare programs and dependents of military personnel. HEW also excluded seniors who had coverage for accidental injury, a single disease or group of diseases, and loss of income.

Another remarkable and rarely acknowledged fact is that although some 40 percent of seniors did not have private health *insurance* in 1962, many had access to health care *services*. It is important to note that health insurance does not equal or guarantee access to health care services. In fact, those who were not "low income" had access to health care—they just paid their doctors without using a third party to administer the transaction.

There were also a number of government programs to help low-income seniors obtain medical care in the 1960s. As discussed previously, the Kerr-Mills program expanded coverage for up to 77 percent of seniors.

The Hill-Burton program was another important safety net for seniors. The Hospital Survey and Construction Act, known as the Hill-Burton Act, was enacted in 1946 to provide federal loans and grants for constructing and improving hospitals. In return, hospital grantees were required to provide free care for 20 years to persons unable to pay for medical services.[16] Many hospitals and other health care facilities were receiving Hill-Burton grants when Medicare was established.[17] Given this safety net, it's no wonder many seniors did not purchase private health insurance. The federal government had essentially guaranteed free hospital care to many low-income seniors between 1946 and 1966.

Kennedy's Push for Hospital Insurance Fails

During the 1960 presidential campaign, Republican candidate Vice President Richard M. Nixon advocated a means-tested health insurance program for the elderly, basically an expansion of Kerr-Mills. His Democratic opponent, Senator John F. Kennedy, criticized Nixon's proposal and promised that his administration would cover all seniors, regardless of their financial status.[18] The fact that Kennedy won the election by a slim margin indicated that there was no clear mandate or overwhelming support for his proposed program.[19]

Even so, in his 1961 State of the Union address, President Kennedy called for a government program to provide hospital insurance to some 14 million Americans over age 65 through Social Security.[20] Soon introduced was the King-Anderson bill, commonly known as Medicare, which established compulsory coverage for hospital and nursing home care for seniors. It did not cover doctor visits. The bill had wide support from labor unions, the American Public Health Association, the American Nursing Association, and liberal seniors' groups, especially the labor-backed National Council of Senior Citizens. The AMA, the Association of American Physicians and Surgeons (AAPS), various business groups, and conservative seniors opposed it.

Kennedy's Medicare bill met numerous obstacles on Capitol Hill. Between 1962 and 1964, hearings were held each year and nearly 14,000 pages of testimony were compiled.[21] But Rep. Mills did not have the votes to report a bill out of the controlling House Ways and Means Committee. Even so, Mills continued working behind the scenes to secure Medicare's future passage. In January 1964, Mills committed to having Blue Cross administer the proposed hospital program. According to a January 27, 1964, memo from President Lyndon Johnson's assistant Larry O'Brien,

> Mills quite forcefully opposes letting the commercial insurance companies in on the act. Labor unions would raise a major howl about the insurance companies. Mills was eager that we begin negotiations at once with Blue Cross.[22]

Meanwhile, powerful lobbying groups were effective in temporarily stopping the King-Anderson version of Medicare (hospital coverage financed under the Social Security system) from being enacted until it was modified to meet their demands. For example, in 1964, when the Committee was deadlocked over Medicare, the AMA persuaded the swing vote, Rep. John C. Watts (D-Ken.), to vote against it.[23] In January 1964, the *Washington Post* published a column by syndicated columnist Drew Pearson suggesting that the AMA had made a deal with tobacco-state congressmen.[24] According to the purported deal, the AMA agreed to investigate further the relationship between tobacco and lung cancer in return for opposition to Medicare by congressmen and senators from tobacco states.[25] (The U.S. Surgeon General's historic report linking smoking to cancer was released in 1964.) Historian Irving Bernstein reported that on February 7, 1964, six leading cigarette companies gave the AMA $10 million to study smoking and health.[26] The AMA's *Digest of Official Actions*, covering 1959–1968, reveals that in 1964 the organization accepted a grant from six major tobacco companies. A year later, according to the *Digest*, the AMA declined to endorse the Surgeon General's report on smoking.[27] This example shows how powerful lobbying groups effectively prevented the early King-Anderson version of Medicare from moving forward.

Johnson Supports Expanded Medicare

Soon after Kennedy's death, President Johnson vowed to make Medicare a priority. The Democrats' landslide election of 1964 significantly increased the likelihood of passing a national health care program. Some people involved in the Medicare debate suggest that public mourning for Kennedy provided Johnson a unique opportunity to pass legislation. Dr. William Ramsey, who served as Field Service Assistant Director of the AMA in the mid-1960s, said, "Guilt over that event [the assassination] caused Congress to pass many programs Kennedy had sought."[28]

In January 1965, during his State of the Union address, Johnson urged Congress to pass Medicare. It has been suggested that Johnson moved fast to rush through as much legislation as he could during his "honeymoon" session in order to exploit the historic moment.[29] The bill, assigned the first number in both the Senate and the House, included coverage for 60 days of hospitalization and 60 days of nursing home care.[30]

The 1965 Medicare bill also included an enticing bonus for seniors: a 7 percent increase in Social Security benefits.[31] Tying Medicare to an increase in benefits was a brilliant political strategy. Seniors had not had an increase since 1959.[32] Thus they were being offered "free" health insurance—even though they had paid nothing into the Medicare hospital trust fund—plus an increase in Social Security benefits. It also placed politicians in a position whereby voting against Medicare would be a vote against an increase in cost-of-living assistance.

The AMA and Republicans Offer Counter Proposals

When it appeared that Medicare would pass, the AMA recommended an alternative bill titled "Eldercare," which would have provided much more coverage than the original Medicare bill, including doctor visits, nursing home care, and prescription drugs. It was basically an enlarged Kerr-Mills program, essentially the same as today's Medicaid. The AMA's counterplan would use Blue Cross/Blue Shield to provide the insurance.[33]

The Republicans sponsored yet another alternative, "Bettercare," which would have established a voluntary insurance program covering doctors' fees, financed by a $3-per-month premium deducted from Social Security benefits and matched by funds from general tax revenues.[34] The AAPS correctly argued that it would discourage seniors from buying private health insurance. Those who wonder how the federal government got seniors to drop their private insurance and join Medicare need look no further.

On March 3, 1965, Chairman Mills, who had opposed Kennedy's Medicare proposal several years, pulled a planned "legislative coup" that would forever change this nation's health care system.[35]

Closed-Door Meetings and Mills' "Three-Layered Cake"

After spending all of February with "a parade of medical lobby groups moving through his closed committee room, probing exhaustively into the detailed operations of hospitals, nursing homes, visiting nurse associations and the like,"[36] Mills surprised nearly everyone by recommending combining all *three* health care proposals: King-Anderson (which became Medicare Part A), "Bettercare" (which became Medicare Part B), and "Eldercare" (which became Medicaid). Wilbur Cohen later reflected on how this sudden change in policy occurred:

> I was the primary [Johnson] Administration representative, seated in the center of a group of Departmental experts at a long table below the great, raised horseshoe table at which sat all the members of the [Ways and Means] Committee. Without any advance notice, Mills asked me why we could not put together a plan that included the Administration's Medicare hospital plan with a broader voluntary plan covering physicians and other services. I answered that it was possible. I had no specific authority from anyone to underwrite such a proposal, but I had enough common sense not to dismiss it out of hand. Then we wrote up the new proposal, virtually overnight. . . . There was no policy clearance with others in the Department [HEW] or in the Budget Bureau or White House. Mills had scored a coup. Johnson immediately realized it. I was the intermediary for a major expansion of our proposal without any intervening review of the details of the proposal as developed by staff. In this case, the federal government was moving into a major area of medical care with practically no review of alternatives, options, trade-offs, or costs.[37]

The expanded Medicare program quickly became known as Mills' "three-layered cake." Although Cohen has indicated that the Johnson White House wasn't aware of Mills' plans to combine the three programs, internal White House documents, obtained from the Lyndon Baines Johnson Library, prove otherwise. In fact, Johnson's special assistant for congressional relations, Larry O'Brien, had briefed the president on Mills' plans as early as January 27, 1964. On that date, O'Brien sent Johnson a memo stating that Mills was planning to combine an expanded Kerr-Mills program (Medicaid) and physician services (Medicare Part B) with the King-Anderson bill (Medicare Part A).[38] On September 23, 1964, O'Brien informed Johnson that Mills was planning on "throwing in the kitchen sink in an attempt to insure the image that this [Medicare] would not be a program under Social Security."[39]

In other words, combining the three programs would make it appear as though Medicare were voluntary and that seniors would have access to private health insurance. Mills himself later confirmed that the idea of combining the three programs was not a spontaneous act but that he had planned it.[40]

Given the complexity of the massive final Medicare proposal—nearly 300 pages long—it is no surprise that even some Democrats reportedly didn't know what was in it. Many deferred to Mills for legislative analysis.[41] The Ways and Means Committee met behind closed doors for two months to discuss the bill. Professor Charlotte Twight points out that because no public hearings were held in the House in 1965, the news media were less able to inform the public about Medicare than they might have been.[42]

A 1965 *Wall Street Journal* editorial reported the reaction around Capitol Hill, noting that following the expansion of the Medicare bill, "Democratic members walked around the House corridors looking very pleased with themselves. 'We've got everything in this bill except transportation expenses for the doctors to go to England, where there's not so much socialized medicine,' laughed one. 'We're going through the AMA checklist and filling in all the blanks,' boasted another."[43]

History professor Sheri I. David writes, "The AMA spent $900,000 to say that Medicare was not enough and that Eldercare was better. Mills took them at their word."[44] While it's common knowledge that organized medicine lobbied ferociously against the hospital insurance program for seniors (Medicare Part A), it is often overlooked that the AMA lobbied *for* the government health care program for low-income people (Medicaid).

As William Pearman and Philip Starr have pointed out, "All interests seemed to be represented in some way. Special interests including hospitals, physicians, the health insurance industry and the drug

Figure 3-1
CONGRESSIONAL VOTES FOR MEDICARE (H.R. 6675)

	House of Representatives April 8, 1965	
	Yea	Nay
Democrats	248	42
Republicans	65	73
Total	313	115
	Senate July 28, 1965	
Democrats	57	7
Republicans	13	17
Total	70	24

SOURCE: Barbara Dreyfuss, "Twenty Years Later: Key Players Reminisce," *The Internist*, March 1985, p. 9.

industry were all accommodated."[45] Medicare supporters often tout a 1965 public opinion poll showing that the vast majority of Americans were behind Medicare. What they don't say is that 77 percent didn't know what was in the bill.[46] Moreover, the poll asked if Americans favored *some* assistance in the financing of medical services.[47] It didn't ask their views on state-controlled medicine or on forcing seniors into a one-size-fits-all government health care program. So we don't really know how seniors felt about the Medicare program as it was enacted because the public wasn't informed about it.

On April 8, 1965, the Mills Medicare bill (H.R. 6675) was passed overwhelmingly by the House, 313 to 115. On July 28, the Senate followed, 70 to 24[48] (see Figure 3-1).

The next day—one day before Medicare was signed into law—President Johnson met with AMA leaders at the White House to assure them that the new law would not interfere with the sacred patient-doctor relationship. The formal statement he read also guaranteed freedom of choice for both doctors and patients.[49]

Johnson promised the AMA that Blue Cross and private insurance carriers would serve as the administrative middlemen under the law; they could define the term "reasonable charges" according to what was customary. "Naturally," Harris writes, "the doctors went for this, because they have great influence with most of those outfits [Blue Cross and private insurance carriers]."[50]

On July 30, 1965, the historic Medicare law was signed at the Truman Presidential Library in Independence, Missouri. Because of Truman's significant role in pushing national health care, Johnson invited him to the signing ceremony. During the live telecast, Johnson awarded Truman the first Medicare card,[51] an irony that escaped notice. For years, Democrats claimed that the purpose of a national health program was to help the poor. Yet the first person to receive a Medicare card was former president Truman—hardly a poor man— who had never contributed a single penny to the Medicare trust fund.

Meanwhile, the fate of Medicare depended on the participation of doctors.

Would Physicians Cooperate?

The AMA's new president, Dr. James Z. Appel, encouraged doctors to cooperate with and not boycott Medicare. In a message in the *Journal of the American Medical Association* (July 5, 1965), Appel wrote, "The [AMA's] preenactment propaganda has been almost entirely devoted to an emotional appeal, with deliberate playing down of facts and realistic appraisals of the effects the legislation will have upon people and our society. We, the medical profession, must evaluate these effects so far as we can anticipate them and continue such evaluation from day to day after the law has been implemented. We must do all we can to develop the good points and all we can to eliminate the bad points of the law. Many of you will challenge this last statement. Undoubtedly, some will never accept it."[52]

However, another physician group cleaved to its support of a free market in medicine and urged doctors to boycott Medicare. The AAPS had consistently opposed it. During a 1965 Senate Finance Committee hearing, AAPS president Dr. E. E. Anthony predicted that Medicare would result in third-party intrusion into the practice of medicine: "Since the government will provide and control hospitalization services and the financing thereof, since the government will control the medical services offered to the aged by financing the subsidization of the insurance carriers responsible therefore, the program is one of outright, unadulterated socialism." Anthony also warned, "The physician's judgment would be open to question by others not responsible for the patient's well-being. His diagnostic and therapeutic decisions would be subject to disapproval by those controlling the expenditure of tax money."[53]

When Medicare was eventually passed, a front-page *New York Times* article explained that Anthony was calling for physicians to withhold their cooperation—without which Medicare could not function.[54]

Who Set Up the Medicare Rules?

The day that Medicare was signed into law, the *Wall Street Journal* reported, "Federal officials are confident that organized medicine, which fought Medicare so vigorously, now will cooperate to make it work well if only because the program offers the doctors assurance of payment from patients who otherwise would be unable to afford their regular fees." The article went on to note, "The AMA has quietly created a committee to help the Social Security Administration set up the program. Its job is to find physicians to advise the government on Medicare's rules and regulations and serve on its high-level advisory panels: The Health Insurance Benefits Advisory Council and the National Medical Review Committee. Yesterday President Johnson held a friendly 'summit session' with a larger group of AMA's top officialdom to smoke the peace pipe, though specifics were not discussed."[55]

Just how large a role did organized medicine have in setting up Medicare? Given the wheeling and dealing that took place behind closed doors, the American public will never know for sure. But we do know that, in effect, the passage of Medicare created the largest government-financed health care program in the world.

Did the medical profession win or lose under Medicare? A study by John Colombotos at Columbia University found that a large number of physicians who were opposed to Medicare before it was enacted switched and accepted it after it became law. For example, in New York State, the proportion in favor of Medicare rose to 70 percent less than a year after it was passed (even before it was implemented), up from 38 percent before it became law.[56]

A 1973 article in the *International Journal of Health Services* noted, "Since its inception, Medicare has served as a source of financial support for hospitals, insurance companies and physicians. It has reinforced the position of these institutions in the delivery of health care, by providing funds to help them either to exclude or to gain control over possible competitors."[57] The article explained that from 1962 until Medicare went into effect in 1966, the Blue Cross Association worked with the Social Security Administration in determining actuarial analysis, preparing administrative measures, and drafting specific provisions for legislative proposals [58]

Public health professor Isadore S. Falk has pointed out that the insurance industry benefited from Medicare in three ways: its insurance patterns were preserved and emulated by law; it achieved relief from difficult and expensive insurance obligations for the aged; and it now had a statutory privilege of functioning as fiscal intermediary for the hospital costs (under Part A) and as insurance carrier for the supplementary medical service costs (under Part B). In other words, insurance companies got to drop seniors from their insurance risk pools while at the same time making lots of money by administering Medicare for the government.[59]

Medicare also helped secure politicians' role in health care. "Medicare heralded enhancement of political job security by creating new and broad-based dependence on government," notes economist and attorney Charlotte Twight.[60]

Clearly, special-interest groups and vote-seeking politicians have gained enormously from Medicare. Organized medicine gained by making sure that doctors' services (Medicare Part B) were financed by general revenue instead of through Social Security payroll taxes. Such financing provided a reliable source of income for many physicians. Unlike the Medicare Part A program that is financed by limited Social Security payroll taxes, Medicare Part B is not scheduled to become insolvent because it is financed primarily by general revenues.

Politicians gained, too, by creating a government program that personally affects a very large and powerful voting constituency. Today, many politicians seek seniors' votes with the promise to expand benefits while at the same time keeping Medicare solvent. History has shown us, however, that such promises are often difficult to keep.

Medicare's history shows us how incremental reformers were successful in first establishing policies at the state level and then

51

shifting to the centralized federal level over time. It also reveals how political manipulation—such as tying the Medicare program to an increase in Social Security benefits—was used to pass a compulsory health insurance program in the United States. Moreover, many members of Congress and the public didn't really understand what the final Medicare bill entailed and how it would work. Would Americans have voted for Medicare if they really knew how it would impact their lives in years to come? Was the public adequately informed about Medicare's true future costs? The following chapter examines this important issue.

4. Did Government Officials Ignore the True Costs of Medicare?

When Medicare was being debated in the 1960s, some citizens and taxpayer groups were concerned that program expenditures might grow out of control. This would occur, they reasoned, because wealthy seniors would likely drop private insurance in favor of Medicare. They argued that taxpayers shouldn't have to foot the bill for wealthy seniors who could afford to pay for their own health insurance. However, Medicare advocates assured the concerned citizens and taxpayer groups that all seniors could easily be covered under Medicare with only a small increase in workers' payroll taxes.

Were the Medicare advocates right? Or were they misleading the public regarding the true costs of Medicare, knowing that once the program was created it would be virtually impossible to disband it, regardless of escalating program costs? This chapter examines the early promises made regarding Medicare costs and whether the early projections have proved to be accurate.

Early Promises about Medicare Costs

Americans were continually reassured throughout the early 1960s that Medicare could easily be financed by a new payroll tax (the Medicare tax) of less than 1 percent of each worker's total income. In fact, Health, Education, and Welfare (HEW) officials in 1965 told Congress that the hospital coverage would require no more than a one-percentage-point increase in the payroll tax for employees, employers, and the self-employed.[1]

HEW Secretary Anthony J. Celebrezze told the Senate Finance Committee in 1965, "The financing of this basic plan [Medicare Part A] is based on very conservative cost estimates." He assured the public that by 1987, total payroll taxes for the hospital insurance program would not exceed 0.8 percent for both workers and employers.[2] Annual costs by the year 2000 would not pass $2.5 billion, HEW officials declared.[3]

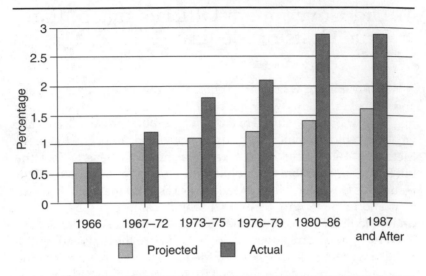

Figure 4-1
PROJECTED VS. ACTUAL MEDICARE TAX BURDEN:
COMBINED EMPLOYEE/EMPLOYER MAXIMUM TAX RATE
FOR FINANCING MEDICARE PART A

SOURCES: U.S. Senate Committee on Finance, "Social Security," Hearings on H.R. 6675, 89–1, April–May 1965; Social Security Administration, "Social Security: Facts and Figures," SSA Publication 05-10011, May 1997.

Sen. Carl T. Curtis (R-Neb.) questioned HEW officials on whether their assumptions were accurate, noting that proposed tax schedules had long been notoriously underestimated. "We by this [Medicare] act," he said, "are determining what our society will pay in social benefits not only next year but ten years from now or fifty years from now. We are determining what the load will be of social benefits for taxpayers that aren't even born yet."[4] The senator's suspicions were right.

Increased Medicare Payroll Taxes

The government has indeed raised the Medicare tax beyond the limit promised. The payroll tax for employees and employers is now nearly double what was projected. Figure 4-1 shows the projected versus the actual tax burden for employees and employers to fund the hospital portion of Medicare (this tax does not finance coverage for most outpatient doctor visits).

Americans were also told that the taxable wage base would be limited to $6,600.[5] Workers would pay Medicare taxes on income up to that amount and no more. However, the wage base has increased over the years, reaching $135,000 in 1993.[6] Then in 1994 the cap on taxable wages was removed altogether (in contrast, Social Security caps the amount of taxable income at $80,400 in 2001).[7] Thus, under Medicare, high-income earners pay high payroll taxes yet receive the same amount of benefits as any other taxpayer.

Medicare Projections: 165 Percent Wrong

In estimating Medicare costs, government actuaries showed just how wrong they could be.

In 1965, federal actuaries projected that the hospital program would grow to only $9 billion by 1990. The program ended up costing more than $66 billion that year. According to Robert J. Myers, chief actuary of the Social Security Administration from 1947 to 1970, the cost of Medicare Part A in constant dollars in 1990 was 165 percent higher than his official estimate. However, former HCFA actuary Guy King explains that Myers' adjustment ignored some Medicare legislation, such as several budget bills, that reduced Medicare expenditures.[8] Thus, the real error in cost estimates is larger than the 165 percent noted by Myers. In 1994 Myers compared the 1990 cost estimate he made in 1965 with the actual results and published the analysis in an article titled "How Bad Were the Original Actuarial Estimates for Medicare's Hospital Insurance Program?" Acknowledging that he missed the mark, he said, "A deviation such as this is nothing to be proud about. . . . Nonetheless, the only thing for me to do now is to commit hari-kari!"[9]

Jokes aside, former Medicare actuaries should examine why their estimates were so far off. Then they should brief current and future actuaries about their miscalculations to prevent future financial glitches. Health policy analysts should look back to see which experts—government actuaries, private actuaries, and so on—have the best track record and are the most reliable for projecting future health care costs.

Just as stockholders demand accurate accounting records from companies they invest in, the American people should demand responsible and accurate financial projections from Medicare. After all, taxpayers and seniors—not unaccountable bureaucrats—are the ones who ultimately pay the price for misleading or intellectually dishonest calculations.

Medicare Part B and General Tax Revenues

When Medicare Part B was created in 1965, HEW officials estimated that half the program would be financed by a $3 monthly premium from seniors (those who enrolled in the voluntary part of the program), with a matching amount from general revenues. In 1967, the first full year the program was up and running, total costs amounted to $1.27 billion.[10]

In 1965, there were no projections made for Part B's long-term costs. Most noteworthy is that Congress failed to establish a budget schedule for Part B expenditures. The National Taxpayers Conference told the Senate Finance Committee in 1965 that little media attention had been paid to this part of the program and that taxpayers were concerned about its effect on general revenues.[11]

The Conference had reason to worry. Seniors' share of premiums quickly grew as a result of the overall rise in Part B expenditures. In fact, Part B spending grew from $1.27 billion to $2.18 billion between 1967 and 1972.[12] In 1972, Congress enacted legislation that limited the annual percentage increase in the Part B premium to the same percentage by which Social Security benefits were adjusted for changes in cost of living (i.e., COLAs). Under that method, revenues from Part B premiums soon dropped from 50 percent to 25 percent of total program revenues. However, starting in the early 1980s, Congress began overriding the COLA limitations by setting the Part B premium level at 25 percent of total Part B program costs.[13] In 2000, Medicare Part B expenditures exceeded $90 billion, with taxpayers financing nearly three-quarters of total costs.[14]

Cost Warnings—Ignored and Unheeded

Astonishingly, during the 1960s, high-ranking government officials were warned that Medicare's future costs would be exorbitant, but they ignored those warnings. They came from Dr. Barkev Sanders, a renowned statistician who for 35 years had conducted health and welfare cost estimates for the federal government and who was responsible for a number of the original cost estimates for Social Security during the 1930s.

Sanders had served as chief of the Division of Health and Disability Studies, Office of the Commissioner of Social Security; research consultant to the Bureau of Old Age and Survivors Insurance; and research consultant to the U.S. Public Health Service. He also was a research analyst with the Commission on Veterans' Pensions and a consultant to the United Mine Workers Welfare and Retirement Fund. Unlike most other critics of the Medicare actuarial estimates, he was *not* opposed to government-financed health care.

Sanders thoroughly examined government projections for Medicare expenditures and concluded they were "far too low." In November 1964 he told *Nation's Business,* a journal of the U.S. Chamber of Commerce, that "the Social Security Administration has been concealing the truth by means of its actuarial estimates."[15] He eventually retired from federal service after failing to get the bureaucrats to use realistic methods for estimating the true cost of Medicare. But his attempt to bring realism to the numbers began before Medicare was created.

In 1959 he critiqued the HEW secretary's report on projected costs for a government hospital program for the aged. He noted that government analysts failed to acknowledge that during the previous 13 years hospital costs had been increasing at a rate two to three times that of wages. Yet federal estimates assumed that the steep increases in hospital costs would disappear in 1960 or would be balanced by an increase in wage rates. Sanders sought permission to conduct studies of what would happen to hospital utilization if Medicare were enacted. He says he was given no encouragement. *Nation's Business* reported, "Subsequently his statistical staff was taken away from him without explanation."[16]

In 1962, Sanders sent a 33-page memorandum to the chief actuary of the Social Security Administration and the commissioner of Social Security explaining that federal cost estimates for Medicare were too low and noting that they included no upward adjustment for increased hospitalization. He noted that the government's low hospital cost estimates would hardly support the claim of dire need on the part of the aged for additional hospital services.[17]

Sanders also pointed out that Medicare cost estimates were based on a 1957 survey that missed 12 percent of the population to be interviewed. "It is quite plausible that many of these might have been missed because they were confined to some medical institution (including short-term hospitals), or had gone to live with relatives because of infirmities," Sanders speculated.[18] He noted that this one deficiency alone, if corrected, would add considerably to the volume of health services. Sanders' findings were based on financial information and statistical analysis that had been available to federal officials for years.

In the 1964 interview with *Nation's Business*, Sanders projected that Medicare would cost at least three times what the bureaucrats estimated and eventually perhaps 10 times as much. "There is every reason to believe that the steeper increase in hospital costs will continue for the foreseeable future. . . . Besides, the faster increasing costs of per diem hospitalization, the growing liberal use of hospital services, as well as the progressive further aging of our aged population, and medical advances over the foreseeable future, would all contribute to this faster upward trend in usage and costs," explained Sanders.[19] He stressed that "if a sound realistic health program cannot be accepted by the public on its merits it should not be imposed on them by the government."[20]

Costs Skyrocket with Passage of Medicare

Medicare was scheduled to take effect July 1, 1966.[21] As early as September 1966, the *New York Times* reported that hospital bills were increasing at a rate five times the cost of living.[22] The newspaper also stressed that following the passage of Medicare, some New York doctors had raised fees for seniors by as much as 300 percent. "Some physicians said that they had raised their fees so that they could accept the government fee as full payment and not attempt to collect the 20 percent from the patients," reported the *New York Times*. A professor of internal medicine explained the increases another way: "I'm not raising fees but eliminating a discount."[23]

By July 1967 President Johnson called for an investigation into rising medical costs. He convened 300 experts to discuss how to lower prices without impairing quality.[24] The panel suggested greater emphasis on the "team approach" in delivering medical care. In effect, this was the beginning of shepherding seniors into managed care.

A 1968 Tax Foundation study found that public spending on medical care had nearly doubled in the first few years of Medicare. The report noted that federal and local governments spent $6.7 billion in 1964 but $12.6 billion in 1967, and private spending increased to $28.8 billion from $24.2 billion. "To date, the major demonstrable effect of the 1965 federal legislation creating Medicare and Medicaid has been a shift in financing medical care from the private to the public sector," the study concluded.[25]

In 1968, President Johnson announced, during a special message to Congress, "Thousands of Americans today are not getting urgently needed medical care because they cannot afford it. . . . The outlook is sobering. It has been estimated that between 1965 and 1975, the cost of living will increase by more than 20 percent. But the cost of health care will increase by nearly 140 percent by 1975:

- Average payments per person will nearly double from about $200 a year to some $400 a year.
- Drug payments will rise by 65 percent.
- Dental bills will climb 100 percent.
- Doctors' bills will climb 160 percent.
- Payments for general hospital services will jump 250 percent."[26]

Johnson went on to say, "Part of these increases will be expanded and improved health services. But a large part of the increase will be unnecessary—a rise which can be prevented." He suggested that we draw on the experience of the newly introduced prepaid health plans that offered incentives for reducing unnecessary hospitalization.[27]

One might think that the increased costs occurred because more seniors were joining the program. However, costs increased much faster than enrollment. According to Yale Professor Theodore Marmor and Robert Wood Johnson Foundation administrator Julie Beglin, in its first five years Medicare spending increased by more than 70 percent, from $4.6 billion in 1967 to $7.9 billion in 1971, while the number of people enrolled grew by only 6 percent, from 19.5 to 20.7 million (see Figure 4-2).[28]

Rise in Surgical Rates

One reason for increased Medicare spending was a rise in surgical expenditures. Government officials had predicted that the development of outpatient care (Medicare Part B) would help reduce overall

Figure 4-2
MEDICARE: THE FIRST FIVE YEARS

Year	Persons Enrolled	Costs (Unadjusted)	Costs (1967-Adjusted Dollars)[29]
1967	19.5 million	$4.6 billion	$4.6 billion
1971	20.7 million	$7.9 billion	$5.6 billion
Change	+ 6%	+ 71%	+ 22%

SOURCE: Ted Marmor and Julie Beglin, "Medicare and How it Grew . . . and Grew . . . and Grew," *Boston Globe*, May 7, 1995.

health care spending, believing that visiting doctors more often would prevent more costly hospitalizations. But the opposite occurred with the creation of Medicare. During the first 10 years of the program, surgical rates increased significantly. The number of surgeries for people 65 and up increased approximately 2½ times, from 6,000 to more than 15,000 for every 100,000 of population.[30]

After 35 Years of Cost Containment Measures, Medicare Spending Still Exceeds General Inflation

For the past 35 years the government has tried many times to bring Medicare (a large portion of overall health spending) in line with the general rise in prices. Those attempts have not succeeded over the long run. There have been temporary successes, but overall Medicare costs (and health care costs in general) have continued to rise at a faster rate than other goods and services. Consequently, health care consumes a greater share of gross domestic product. In 1965 it accounted for just 5.9 percent of national spending.[31] It has now increased to nearly 14 percent of GDP (see Figure 4-3).[32]

President Johnson increased Medicare payroll taxes and the taxable wage base to finance the rising Medicare costs in the late 1960s. The Nixon administration took another route: it imposed price controls on the health sector (as well as other sectors) of the economy.[33] The federal government also adopted a policy known as "Certificate of Need" in the 1970s. This was a central planner's dream.

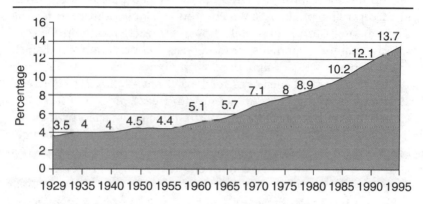

Figure 4-3
NATIONAL HEALTH EXPENDITURES AS PERCENTAGE OF
GROSS NATIONAL PRODUCT (GNP) AND
GROSS DOMESTIC PRODUCT (GDP)
1929–1995

SOURCES: Bureau of the Census, *Historical Statistics of the United States: Colonial Times to 1970, Bicentennial Edition, Part 1* (Washington: Government Printing Office, 1975); Bureau of the Census, *Statistical Abstract of the United States, 1996* (Washington: Government Printing Office, 1996); Katharine Levit et al., "Health Spending in 1998: Signals of Change," *Health Affairs* 19, no. 1 (January/February 2000).

NOTE: The figure shows national health expenditures as a percentage of gross national product (GNP) between 1929 and 1955; other years' national health expenditures are reported as a percentage of gross domestic product (GDP).

The "Certificate of Need" required states' approval for the building of new health care facilities. Under this program, hospitals had to demonstrate a need for expansion before new construction could begin.[34] The decade also brought the HMO Act of 1973, which mandated that employers with 25 or more employees offer workers a health maintenance organization (HMO) plan as an option.[35] Very early attempts to enroll seniors in HMOs were unsuccessful, and Medicare costs continued to rise in the 1970s.[36]

Medicare Growth Slowed for the First Time in History

During the 1980s, the Reagan administration introduced the Prospective Payment System for hospitals, which reimburses hospitals according to a fixed price schedule based on Diagnostic Related Groups (DRGs). For example, a hospital would receive a fixed price for a certain operation performed on a Medicare beneficiary. The DRG system was implemented to create competition among hospitals. In the short term, the DRG policy seemed to slow the growth of Medicare hospital costs, which grew at single-digit rates for the first time in history.[37] Hospitals, however, reacted to the price controls by qualifying patients for more tests and procedures and shifting patients to DRG designations with higher fees.[38]

Cost-containment measures for Part B have failed too. Between 1984 and 1986 there was an attempt to freeze physician fees. The Congressional Budget Office found that doctors reacted by increasing volume. Both hospitals and physicians figured out ways to get around price controls and efforts to reduce hospital utilization. As a result, Part B spending continued to rise on average about 10 percent per year during the 1980s and 1990s.[39]

During the 1990s, President Clinton and Congress implemented policies to reduce Medicare costs by limiting the growth in annual payments for all providers, establishing a prospective payment system for nursing home care, and transferring a significant portion of home health spending from Part A to Part B.[40] They also authorized the creation of a new Medicare + Choice program to encourage seniors to enroll in managed care plans. However, as discussed in Chapter 1, the number of plans serving Medicare beneficiaries has been reduced over the past few years due to complicated federal regulations. No medical savings account plans have been offered under the so-called Medicare + Choice program. In addition, over the past few years, President Clinton and Congress increased federal spending on Medicare fraud and abuse activities, recovering some $1.6 billion in 1998.[41] More recently, the Department of Justice reported recoveries of more than $840 million in 2000 related to health care fraud.[42]

Over the past 30 years, the federal government has raised payroll taxes, expanded the Medicare payroll tax base, capped prices, and shifted costs from one part of the program to the other to keep Medicare solvent. Some of these interventions have helped slow the rate of growth in the short term. However, Medicare spending continues to show unsustainable levels over the long term. Given expected future changes in demographics, Medicare will require major reform during the next decade. If health care costs continue to rise with fewer workers to finance the program, the federal government will have to raise taxes, increase seniors' out-of-pocket costs, reduce seniors' benefits, or implement a combination of these reforms.

Taxpayers should consider carefully how Medicare has affected seniors over the past 35 years, as discussed in the following chapter, in order to forecast the most likely outcomes from future Medicare reforms.

5. How Has Medicare Affected Seniors?

It is well established that Medicare has had a significant impact on our nation's health care costs. But how has the program affected seniors' lives? Are seniors living longer because of Medicare or was life expectancy increasing long before the government got involved? Do seniors have more choices and privacy regarding medical care today? Or has Big Brother invaded their medical and home privacy as a result of Medicare?

The Medicare program has had several important and unintended consequences that should be investigated by policymakers, academicians, the media, and the public at large.

Seniors' Life Expectancy before and after Medicare

It is generally believed that Americans are living longer because of the Medicare program. Indeed, some supporters argue that life expectancy for the elderly in the United States is higher than in any industrialized country in the world (except for Japan) as a result of Medicare.[1] However, a recent *Health Affairs* article points out that at age 60, life expectancy in the United States is similar to the median life expectancy of 28 other industrialized countries.[2] In terms of relative ranking, the United States ranked in the 55th percentile for life expectancy at age 60 for males; and in the 45th percentile for life expectancy at age 60 for females (a percentile rank of 100 represents the highest value).

Today, America devotes a far greater share of national income to medical care than any major industrialized nation—13.5 percent of gross domestic product, compared with about 10 to 11 percent for Germany and France and about 7 to 8 percent for Japan and the United Kingdom.[3] Yet our life expectancy is not much better, as indicated in Table 5-1. Moreover, when adjusted for disabilities, life expectancy in the United States falls slightly below the median rates of the other industrialized countries.[4]

Table 5-1
HEALTH CARE INDICATORS, 1998:
UNITED STATES VS. COMPETITOR NATIONS

Country	Health Expenditures as % GDP	Per Capita Health Expenditures	Life Expectancy at Birth Male	Life Expectancy at Birth Female	Life Expectancy at Age 60** Male	Life Expectancy at Age 60** Female
Canada	9.5%	$2,312	75.8*	81.4*	20.0*	24.2*
France	9.6	$2,077	74.6	82.2	20.0*	25.2*
Germany	10.6	$2,424	74.5	80.5	19.0	23.3
Japan	7.6	$1,822	77.2	84.0	21.0	26.4
Netherlands	8.6	$2,070	75.2	80.7	18.5	23.0
United Kingdom	6.7	$1,461	74.6*	79.7*	18.8*	22.6*
United States	13.6	$4,178	73.9	79.4	19.6	23.1

SOURCE: Organization for Economic Cooperation and Development, *OECD Health Data 2000* (Paris: OECD, 2000); cited in Gerard Anderson and Peter Sotir Hussey, "Comparing Health System Performance in OECD Countries," *Health Affairs* 20, no. 3 (May/June 2001): pp. 219–232.

* 1997 data.

** Expectation of additional years of life at age 60.

Table 5-2
U.S. LIFE EXPECTANCY AT AGE 60: 1930, 1960, AND 1990
(in Total Years)

Race and Gender	1930*	1960	1990
Black Female	74.2	77.7	80.6
White Female	76.1	79.7	83.0
Black Male	73.2	74.9	76.2
White Male	74.7	75.9	78.9

SOURCES: Bureau of the Census, *Historical Statistics of the United States: Colonial Times to 1970, Bicentennial Edition, Part 1* (Washington: Government Printing Office, 1975), p. 56; U.S. National Center for Health Statistics, *Vital Statistics of the United States*, annual (1993); and unpublished data.
*1929–1931 data.

Federal Reserve Chairman Alan Greenspan told the National Bipartisan Commission on the Future of Medicare that Americans spend proportionately more on health care than other industrial countries because the salaries of doctors and other medical providers are higher.[5] He also said that other developed countries have fewer doctors per capita and less modern equipment. "Almost certainly," Greenspan added, "our system produces the most sophisticated, and perhaps the highest quality, medical care in the world. But we have little evidence that, as a result, our population is any healthier, on average, than those populations that devote fewer resources to health care, recognizing, of course, that health outcomes depend on a host of other influences in addition to the level of medical expenditures."[6]

Medicare supporters also tout increases in life expectancy over the past 30 years as evidence that government health care works. However, they rarely reveal that average life expectancy was on the rise long before Medicare was enacted. In fact, average life expectancy in the United States increased from 47.3 years to 69.7 years between 1900 and 1960.[7]

It is important to note that life expectancy was low in the early 1900s primarily because of high infant mortality rates. The large number of infant deaths made the overall life expectancy rate appear low. However, in the early 1900s, those who reached age 60 typically lived at least another 10 years or more. Life expectancy for seniors had been increasing before Medicare was enacted in the United States. Table 5-2 shows historical trends in life expectancy for those who reach age 60. We can't attribute the increases in seniors' life expectancy to Medicare when in fact such growth had occurred long before the federal government began footing their health care bills.

A recent comparison of international health statistics concluded that since 1960, U.S. *relative* performance (compared to that of 28 industrialized countries) on most health indicators declined; on none did it improve from 1960 to 1998.[8] It is important to note that during the past century, life expectancy had been increasing worldwide, not just in the United States. Thus, since 1960 our relative ranking on most health indicators has slipped in international comparisons. This could possibly represent improvements in other countries' health systems. Given that many factors affect health outcomes—including lifestyle habits and socioeconomic factors—one cannot determine conclusively the reasons for those trends. However, it is clear that U.S. life expectancy was on the rise long before Medicare was enacted, and, although overall life expectancy continues to improve, our relative ranking has declined over the past 30 years.

Was Medicare the Main Factor in Reducing Poverty among Seniors?

Considering that Congress gave no Social Security cost-of-living increases to seniors between 1959 and 1965, it is no wonder seniors' income fell well below the national average during that period. Congress refrained from increasing seniors' benefits until they added a 7 percent Social Security increase to the proposed Medicare bill in 1965. The National Academy of Social Insurance reports that most of the income gains for the elderly that occurred during the 1970s were attributable, in large part, to legislated increases in Social Security benefits. The Academy reports:

> Congress enacted *ad hoc* benefit increases that took effect in 1970, 1971, 1972 and 1974, and then indexed benefits to keep pace with inflation. Between 1969 and 1983 median total incomes of the elderly grew about 50 percent. Since 1983, median incomes of the elderly have grown somewhat slower than for most younger household types. . . . Rising cash incomes during the 1970s brought many of the elderly out of poverty. In 1966, 28.5 percent of elderly Americans were poor—nearly twice the rate for the population as a whole (14.7 percent) and much higher than the rate for children under age 18 (17.6 percent). By 1982, after the real increase in

Figure 5-1
ELDERLY (65 AND OVER) LIVING IN POVERTY (Percentage)

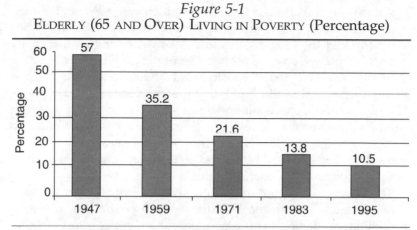

SOURCES: *Economic Report of the President* (Washington: Government Printing Office, 1964); *Older Americans 2000: Key Indicators of Well-Being* (Washington: Federal Interagency Forum on Aging Related Statistics, 2000).

> Social Security benefits mentioned above, the elderly poverty rate was below that for the population as a whole, and it has remained there since. In 1996, the poverty rate for the elderly was 11 percent. In contrast, the poverty rate for children under 18 rose and exceeded 20 percent during most of the 1990s.[9]

Supporters claim that many seniors were lifted out of poverty because of Medicare.[10] However, they overlook the fact that seniors' poverty rate was on the decline *before* Medicare was created (see Figure 5-1). In fact, the percentage of seniors in poverty declined from 57 percent in 1947 to 35.2 percent in 1959.[11] Those who claim Medicare is responsible for lifting seniors out of poverty should consider the important role of Social Security cash benefit increases.

Today's Seniors Are Paying Nearly as Much Out of Pocket as They Were before Medicare

A major reason Medicare was needed, argued supporters, was to reduce seniors' out-of-pocket health care expenses. However, Medicare did not achieve that goal because health care costs increased much faster than federal actuaries had estimated. And since Medicare requires seniors to pay deductibles, and co-payments, their out-of-pocket costs go up whenever hospital and doctor fees rise.

69

Within one year after Medicare was implemented, Walter Reuther, a national union leader and president of the United Automobile Workers, told the House Ways and Means Committee that many retired people were worse off because of new billing practices.[12] In 1967 the *New York Times* reported that Medicare was paying less than half the total health care bills for some seniors.[13] Dr. James G. Haughton, first deputy administrator of New York City's Health Services Administration, told the *Times* that because of quirks in Medicare, some people were paying more for certain medical services than they had paid before the plan started and this kept some people, especially the poor, from buying health care.[14]

The trend in high out-of-pocket costs continued over the next three decades. In January 1971 the Senate Committee on Aging reported that Medicare was paying less than half of seniors' health bills.[15] In 1985 Rep. Claude Pepper (D-Fla.) reported that Medicare beneficiaries were paying 20 percent of their income for health care, the same as in 1964—the year before Medicare was passed.[16]

All told, Medicare co-payments and deductibles have grown from $4.5 billion in 1977 to $26.8 billion in 1996, an average annual rate of change of 9.9 percent.[17] That does not include spending on nursing home care and other long-term care services.

In 2000, an American Association of Retired Persons study estimated that, on average, Medicare beneficiaries spend about $2,510— or 19 percent of income—on out-of-pocket health care costs.[18] That figure includes spending on payments for Medicare deductibles and coinsurance, prescription drugs, dental care, and Part B and private insurance premiums. It does not include spending for home care or long-term nursing care. The out-of-pocket estimate would be much higher if it included those costs. (As described below, nursing home care alone costs approximately $56,000 per year.)[19]

The future doesn't look any better for tomorrow's seniors. According to Marilyn Moon, senior fellow at the Urban Institute, seniors' share of income devoted to health care is expected to reach 28.6 percent by 2025, up from 19.1 percent in 1965 (see Figure 5-2).[20]

By a broader measure of health care spending, the Medicare program covers only about half of seniors' total spending for medical services. In 1997, total average spending on medical services was $9,340 per beneficiary. Medicare paid $5,114 per beneficiary (55 percent). The remaining was paid for out of pocket, by private insurance, Medicaid, or other sources (see Figure 5-3).

Figure 5-2
ACUTE HEALTH SPENDING BY THE ELDERLY
(Percentage of Income)

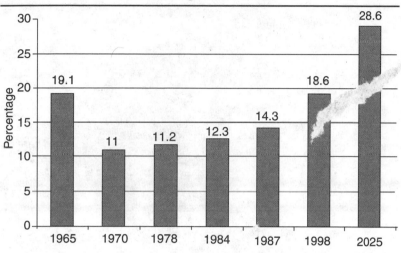

SOURCE: Marilyn Moon, The Urban Institute, "Medicare Matters: The Value of Social Insurance," Testimony before the U.S. Senate Committee on Finance, May 27, 1999.

NOTE: The 2025 figure is projected.

Medicare clearly has not met its purported goal of reducing seniors' out-of-pocket spending on health care. Rather, the program has led to skyrocketing costs for all seniors. Today's seniors might have been better served if the free market had been allowed to work and a safety net had been provided for those too poor to pay for health care.

Seniors Face Huge Long-Term Care Costs

One reason that seniors must pay huge out-of-pocket expenses for medical care is that Medicare does not cover catastrophic illnesses. Unlike most employer-sponsored health insurance, Medicare does not cap the amount one must pay for health care in any given year. That is why 39,840 seniors had an average cost-sharing liability of $22,124 in 1997.[21] They had to pay that amount either out of pocket or through supplemental insurance.

Figure 5-3
SOURCES OF PAYMENT FOR MEDICARE BENEFICIARIES' USE OF MEDICAL SERVICES, 1997

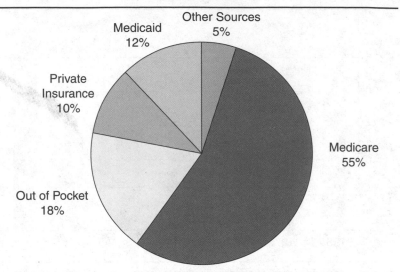

SOURCE: HCFA/Office of Strategic Planning; data are from the Medicare Current Beneficiary Survey, July 2000.

NOTE: Beneficiary out-of-pocket spending does not include seniors' payments for Medicare Part B premiums, private insurance premiums, or HMO premiums.

Consequently, an estimated 75 percent of seniors have some type of supplemental insurance. An additional 12 percent of low-income seniors qualify for Medicaid, the government program for the poor, and another 2 percent of seniors have some form of supplemental insurance that is not identified as private insurance or Medicaid. However, 11 percent of the aged have neither supplemental insurance nor Medicaid coverage and are at full risk for Medicare's cost-sharing liability.[22]

Seniors Face Expensive Nursing Home and Home Care Costs

Many Americans are unaware that Medicare covers only a limited amount of nursing home and home care. Of course, one might maintain that Medicare should not pay for such services, because they constitute living expenses and not medical care expenses. However, instead of deciding between paying out of pocket for their long-term care needs (e.g., nursing homes, home health care, etc.) and purchasing private insurance to cover most of those costs, many citizens believe that Medicare will cover those expenses. When they turn 65, they will be surprised to discover that even though they have been paying Medicare taxes throughout their working years, the program will not cover routine nursing home care unless it is related to hospitalization or other urgent medical treatment. Those who need to go into nursing homes will find that the average cost is about $56,000 a year.[23] In 1997, about 4.3 percent of the U.S. population age 65 and older resided in nursing homes.[24] Nearly three-fourths of the nursing home residents were women.

Nursing home costs are projected to increase to $97,000 per year (in 1996 dollars) by 2030, and by that year total expenditures for nursing home care could reach $330 billion. The American Council of Life Insurance notes, "To put this number into perspective, nursing home expenditures in 2030 will equal the size of the entire Social Security system today."[25]

Americans spent approximately $134 billion on long-term care in 1999.[26] Medicare and Medicaid together paid for nearly 58 percent of long-term care (other public programs paid for 3 percent). Many retirees have to spend their life savings and then turn to Medicaid to pay for this care. Consequently, Medicaid has become one of the fastest-growing programs in state budgets, with long-term care accounting for about a third of total annual Medicaid expenditures.[27]

The remaining 39 percent of the long-term care bill was paid for privately, either by private insurance or out of pocket. Less than 10 percent of seniors carry long-term care insurance. Consequently, in 1999 seniors and their families paid some $33.5 billion out of pocket for nursing home and home care (25 percent of all long-term care expenditures).[28] Government officials rarely factor those amounts into the final calculation when determining seniors' out-of-pocket expenses for health care.

Medicare and Medicaid Help Fill Empty Nursing Home Beds

There is no doubt that the passage of the 1965 Medicare law (which also authorized the Medicaid program) facilitated the institutionalization of the nation's elderly. A 1965 front-page *Wall Street Journal* article reported that, prior to the 1965 law, nursing homes were losing profits because of too many empty beds:

> Some 115,000 nursing home beds are now empty, more than double the 55,000 vacancies five years ago. Says an administrator of a 70-bed south-side Chicago facility that competes with a dozen other homes in its immediate area: "It's been real tough. We've only been about half full since the home opened three years ago." An occupancy rate of at least 70% is usually considered necessary for profitable operation.[29]

The article also noted that some nursing home administrators were counting on the Johnson administration's Medicare program to ease their plight by enabling more seniors to use their facilities.

Nursing home administrators got their wish and the federal government helped finance care at many of the 5,076 new facilities established between 1963 and 1971.[30] Nursing home costs increased significantly. The *average* per-family out-of-pocket expenditure rose from $287 to $1,194 per year (in 1991 dollars) between 1961 and 1991.[31] One might think that higher costs would deter seniors from entering nursing homes. But seniors unable to care for themselves at home, or without resources and family to care for them at home, don't have any other option but to seek institutional care.

Women in particular should take a close look at the consequences of the Medicare program's approach to long-term care. They are more likely than men to require long-term care in a nursing home and currently represent nearly two-thirds of the nursing home population. This trend is projected to continue. A report from the U.S. Census Bureau found that the number of centenarians has nearly doubled during the 1990s, reaching an estimated 70,000 in 1999. Four out of five are women. Life expectancy is expected to increase, with the centenarian population reaching 834,000 by 2050.[32]

In 1960, U.S. census data found that 470,000 citizens were in institutions for the aged.[33] At the beginning of the 21st century the figure is about 1.5 million people, with projected growth to 5 million by 2040.[34] At the same time, there will be fewer working taxpayers—relative to the number of Medicare beneficiaries—available to pick up the costs of seniors' long-term care either through Medicare or Medicaid assistance. Thus tax rates will have to be raised or services and quality of care reduced.

A General Accounting Office (GAO) study found that one in four nursing homes has serious deficiencies.[35] Even after sanctions, 40 percent of the homes with severe deficiencies were in violation three years later.[36] The problem will only get worse when there are fewer workers to pay for long-term care.

During the 1960s, when Medicare was a new idea, the American people didn't realize what coverage would be guaranteed—and many still don't realize it today. A survey taken in January 1965 and circulated in Congress found that most Americans believed that Medicare would cover more services than it actually did.[37] Clearly, a gap existed between what Medicare was expected to cover and what it actually covered. Economist and attorney Charlotte Twight explains, "The gulf between what the public thought and what was actually in the [Medicare] bill was enormous. The most pressing rationale for compulsory health insurance continually put forward by government officials and echoed by the public was the specter that responsible older people could be ruined financially by catastrophic illness. Yet neither the 1963 nor the 1965 proposal [which became Medicare law] provided coverage for catastrophic illness."[38]

Many people haven't been well informed about the intricacies of Medicare. They continue handing over 2.9 percent of their incomes (combined employee-employer Medicare payroll tax) thinking they will have coverage for catastrophic illness and long-term care during retirement. They're often shocked to find they must spend their life savings to qualify for coverage through Medicaid. By creating an illusion that seniors will be taken care of during old age, Medicare actually encourages taxpayers to become dependent on an inadequate catastrophic illness and long-term care program.

Wouldn't it make more sense for people to invest in insurance for catastrophic illness and long-term care that they can carry into retirement? Wouldn't seniors be better off if they had purchased such policies when they were younger and the premiums were affordable? In effect, Medicare has absorbed tax dollars that preempted alternative uses of resources that could have—and some might argue should have—been used to purchase private long-term care protection.

Has Medicare Created an Efficient Insurance System for Seniors?

Medicare is a pay-as-you-go system in which the government collects money from taxpayers and uses it to pay part of seniors' medical bills. It does so by contracting with 60 insurance companies to process claims for some 39 million Americans.[39] All told, Blue Cross and Blue Shield plans process about 90 percent of Part A claims and about 57 percent of Part B claims under fee-for-service Medicare.[40]

Medicare proponents often claim that it is an efficient program. Yet waste, fraud, and abuse cost taxpayers $11.9 billion a year[41]—more than $32 million dollars per day. Some health policy analysts point out that this figure may be overstated because inadvertent mistakes—such as improper coding of claims—are considered fraud.

Nevertheless, in July 1999 the GAO released a study showing that contractors hired to spot Medicare fraud were themselves implicated in wrongdoing and had been forced to pay at least $235 million in civil and criminal penalties since 1993.[42] The *New York Times* reported that during a two-year period, 4 of the 44 companies that run Medicare's day-to-day financial operations—in California, Colorado, Illinois, and New Mexico—pleaded guilty to criminal fraud charges.[43] The GAO has concluded that the federal government sets few standards for evaluating Medicare contractors and rarely questions their performance, in part because federal employees have "cozy" relationships with some of the Medicare contractors.[44] The GAO also found that some contractors had filed false claims, destroyed thousands of claims to reduce the backlog of work, and even turned off the telephones when they couldn't answer customers' calls in the prescribed amount of time.[45]

However, the federal government has become quite zealous in its efforts to crack down on other kinds of Medicare fraud and abuse. The Federal Bureau of Investigation and the Justice Department have joined forces with the American Association of Retired Persons (AARP) to curb such activity. The federal government and AARP are asking seniors to report their doctors if they suspect fraud, such as "performing inappropriate or unnecessary services" or "routinely waiving patient coinsurance."[46] This heavy-handed approach will ultimately harm the patient-doctor relationship.

The federal government doesn't want seniors to control their health spending ostensibly because it fears doctors might defraud them in the marketplace. Yet there don't appear to be major problems with fraud and abuse in sectors of health care where patients pay out of pocket for care, such as for eyeglasses or dental care. In those sectors, patients have an incentive to become aware of costs and benefits. Empowering consumers and encouraging them to become cost-conscious is a much better approach than the government's heavy-handed anti-fraud crusade.

Medicare sometimes classifies services it doesn't want to pay for as "improper" claims—grouping those services in the fraud, waste, and abuse category. Yet, having individuals pay directly for more of their health care could reduce the need for the federal government to act as the judge in deciding what services are "medically necessary" (i.e., proper). Clearly, Medicare's one-size-fits-all coverage policy doesn't meet the needs of each and every senior—including millions of competent seniors who are more than capable of making personal health care decisions for themselves.

Medicare Restricts Choice

One of the most disturbing problems with Medicare is that it restricts seniors' choice of health insurance and their right to pay privately for health care. Since seniors are automatically enrolled in Medicare Part A, they are subject to hundreds of thousands of pages of rules and regulations without their consent.[47] In 1997, Congress enacted Section 4507 of the Balanced Budget Act of 1997. That provision says that before any doctor can accept private payments from Medicare-participating seniors for Medicare-covered services, the provider must promise not to accept Medicare payments from *all* Medicare-participating seniors for two years.[48] The United Seniors Association challenged the provision in federal court, but the court ducked the question of the section's constitutionality. The court clarified, however, that seniors are free to pay privately for services *not* covered by Medicare.[49]

Members of Congress from both parties claim that Section 4507 gives seniors more choices than they had under the old law, in which HCFA harassed doctors who attempted to contract privately with seniors, even though a federal judge found nothing in the law that prohibited private contracting. But there is a catch with the new law.

The only way doctors get relief from HCFA harassment is if they stop seeing Medicare patients for two years. This provision hardly gives seniors more choice of doctors. Moreover, according to statutory language, only Medicare-participating doctors of medicine and osteopathy are relieved from HCFA harassment. Other Medicare-participating providers (chiropractors, dentists, optometrists, podiatrists, and other types of doctors) are denied the legal right to contract with Medicare patients.

Why should Americans be concerned about this new restriction? Because every year millions of seniors seek medical treatment from chiropractors, dentists, optometrists, and podiatrists, who are reimbursed for certain services under Medicare. According to the most recently available HCFA data, in 1998 chiropractors served 1.4 million Medicare beneficiaries, dentists (oral surgeons) served 87,920, optometrists served 3.9 million, and podiatrists served 5.1 million.[50] All told, these doctors provided more than 47 million services for Medicare patients in 1998.

Opponents of private contracting claim it would increase Medicare fraud and abuse. However, allowing seniors to contract privately for health care and insurance could actually reduce fraud because the private health insurance industry could not afford to tolerate the level of misconduct that has proved typical of the Medicare program.

Medicare Invades Seniors' Privacy

Why would anyone wish to pay privately for medical services covered under Medicare? Perhaps to protect their privacy. Under Medicare rules established in 1999, millions of seniors may soon find government officials poring over their most private medical records without their consent. The medical-privacy threat comes from a new data-collection system being implemented by HCFA.

A new program titled the Outcome and Assessment Information Set (OASIS) was established to monitor the quality of home health agencies delivering care to Medicare patients. However, in an attempt to monitor care delivered to seniors in their homes, the government program requires all patients receiving home health care, including non-Medicare patients, to divulge personal medical, sexual, and psychological information. Government contractors—mainly home health nurses—are directed to record such things as whether a senior has expressed "depressive feelings" or has used "excessive profanity."[51]

Even more alarming, the government is also collecting information on caregivers, including husbands, wives, children, and anyone else who assists in caring for seniors in their homes. Homebound seniors have no option regarding their privacy. If they refuse to share medical and lifestyle information, their health care workers are required to act as informants. This means total strangers will be permitted to speak for seniors.

The OASIS data collection policy went into effect in 1999.[52] Under this policy, extremely detailed and fully identifiable information will eventually be turned over to state and federal governments.[53]

Medicare officials try to assure the public that the federal government protects patients' privacy. However, the GAO reported to Congress that at 5 of 12 Medicare contractors' sites in 1998, auditors were able to penetrate security and obtain sensitive Medicare information.[54] The GAO also reported that an HCFA employee had been accessing Medicare beneficiary files more frequently than appeared necessary for performing his job.

When approached about the possible violation of confidentiality, the employee admitted he looked through the files of famous people.[55] Even if this is an anomaly, when it comes to medical privacy, it is difficult to compensate for invasions of privacy. Government simply cannot take back leaked information or easily repair damaged reputations.

Medicare Paves the Way for a National Health Information System

Currently, the federal government is fostering the creation of a national health information system. The purported purpose is to improve the efficiency of the Medicare program (the nation's largest purchaser of health care) and the health care system in general. Congressional authority for the forthcoming system was tucked away in a bill signed into law over five years ago. The Health Insurance Portability and Accountability Act of 1996 (HIPAA) includes a provision titled "Administrative Simplification."[56] This section of HIPAA is quite similar to a section of President Clinton's Health Security Act proposed in 1993.

HIPAA's Administrative Simplification section requires that a "unique health identifier" be assigned to every (a) health care provider, (b) health plan, (c) individual, and (d) employer to be used for health care claims that are processed electronically. However, due to enormous public outcry, plans to assign every American a unique health identifier have been put on hold temporarily—at least until strong federal privacy protections are in place.

A HIPAA-mandated final federal medical privacy rule was promulgated by President Clinton in December 2000 and endorsed by President Bush in April 2001 (although he has modified it somewhat). Unfortunately, the final rule (in its promulgated version) does not offer individuals the ability to control the privacy of their personal health information.[57] Instead, the rule gives the federal government the authority to determine who can access patients' medical records without their permission. At the same time, it places undue financial and management burdens on providers to comply with the rule. The final medical privacy rule is likely going to be modified during the next few years. In the meantime, other HIPAA-mandated regulations will be fully implemented, including requirements for identifiers, rules for coding medical claims processed electronically, and security standards for computerized databases storing electronic medical records.

It is important to realize that federal laws intended to make Medicare more efficient are often drafted to apply to all citizens, whether or not they are eligible for Medicare. HIPAA is a clear example. Every American patient—young and old alike—and provider is now going to have to abide by the complicated and ineffectual federal medical privacy rule in order to try to improve Medicare's inefficiencies.

The Medicare Appeals Process Is Slow

Another reason that seniors would pay privately for services is that Medicare does not make clear what it covers under all circumstances. Many patients and doctors have to speculate how HCFA would rule on a coverage decision. When patients are forced to challenge denied claims through the bureaucratic appeals process, they may incur sizable legal expenses.

Federal officials told Congress that in 1998 an initial ruling on a disputed hospital claim took about 52 days. An average appeal took 310 days. Disputes over Medicare Part B denied claims took even longer. On average, in 1998 it took 116 days for an in-house appeal decision and 524 days for an appeal decision from a Social Security administrative law judge.[58] For elderly Americans, the length of time involved in Medicare appeals can mean a matter of life and death.

Robert Moffit of the Heritage Foundation notes that Medicare denies some 24 percent of all Medicare Part B claims.[59] Because Americans do not have an enforceable contract with the federal government, there is no guarantee that tomorrow's Medicare will cover the benefits that taxpayers think they are contributing to today.

Scarce Medicare Funds Are Used to Pay for Training Doctors

Many taxpayers, meanwhile, don't know that their Medicare tax dollars are used to train physicians. The federal government, primarily Medicare, is the single largest source of financial support for graduate medical education. Medicare paid $7.1 billion for doctor training in 1998.[60] The federal government began paying a significant portion of the cost of training medical interns and residents when Medicare was passed. Congress authorized subsidies for graduate medical education through Medicare out of a concern in 1965 that there were too few physicians to handle the newly covered seniors.[61]

The use of limited Medicare funds to train doctors has been criticized. In response, Congress passed a provision, in the Balanced Budget Act of 1997, to pay hospitals *not* to train as many physicians.[62] This is an example of being so dependent on federal dollars that a subsidy must continue even when the "crisis," an undersupply of physicians, has passed.

Some critics have suggested that the financial burden of training doctors should be spread evenly among all taxpayers. A task force supported by the Commonwealth Fund recommended assessing the payers for nearly everyone who uses—or may use—the health care system. It recommended financing medical education through mandated contributions from Medicare, Medicaid, all private payers, or from the allocation of general revenues.[63]

The supply of qualified physicians and other providers should be determined in the marketplace, not by a central government agency or special interest groups. It is ironic that when it comes to freezing Medicare payments, organized medicine is the first to say, "Let the market work." Yet, at the same time, it continues to lobby heavily for federal funding to train doctors.

We should encourage doctors to follow other professions and pay their own way for education and training. There is little reason for Medicare to continue funding the training of medical residents. If

Medicare stopped subsidizing medical schools, they would suddenly have a strong incentive to find more innovative and cost-effective ways to train doctors, and the medical schools would compete more aggressively on the basis of quality and price.

Conclusions

Any debate about Medicare must take a hard look at the program's effects on seniors in terms of coverage, costs, choice, and privacy. Policymakers, academicians, the media, and the public alike should carefully examine historical trends in life expectancy and health care costs dating back to the 1900s. Since conditions had been improving long before Medicare, it is misleading to give the program full credit for improvements after 1965. A more pressing task is a thorough examination of Medicare's many unintended consequences, and their implications for future changes.

6. Reforming Medicare in the 21st Century: Time for True Choice and Competition

Given the enormous problems facing Medicare, the question of how best to restructure it will take center stage in the new millennium. Medicare's history shows that even with all the tinkering around the edges during the past 35 years, the program continues to leave many seniors without adequate catastrophic coverage for illnesses during old age. Older persons, especially older women, are filing for bankruptcy because of high out-of-pocket medical costs.[1] And although Medicare was created to reduce seniors' out-of-pocket costs, today's seniors continue to pay, as a percentage of their income, as much out of pocket as they did when Medicare was created.

Until recently, many seniors haven't complained about paying significant copayments, deductibles, and out-of-pocket expenses under Medicare because a large number of them didn't pay Medicare payroll taxes for many years. In fact, when Medicare was enacted in 1965, nearly all seniors qualified for "free" hospital care (Medicare Part A) even though they had not paid a single penny into the program. Consequently, over the years many seniors have willingly accepted Medicare's limited coverage and rather significant copayment and deductible requirements. After all, why should they complain about the program if they hadn't paid much (in terms of payroll taxes) to support Medicare?

Today's retirees are quite different. They have been paying taxes to support Medicare for more than 35 years. When they retire, they may believe that they deserve comprehensive medical care, especially since they feel they have paid for it.[2] Moreover, they already have become accustomed to employer-sponsored health insurance coverage that shielded them during their working lives from the true price of health care services. Whenever people rely on third parties—whether it's employers or government agencies—to pay

83

for their medical care, they consume more services than they would if they were paying a greater share of the costs on their own.

Tomorrow's seniors—the baby boomers—also have little experience as cost-conscious health care consumers. They may be even less likely than current retirees to accept rationed care from the government during their later years. They also aren't going to want to pay high copayments and deductibles after already paying Medicare taxes their entire working lives. Although the compulsory feature of Medicare Part A has for the most part remained unchallenged, that is likely to change in the coming years as a large number of free-spirited baby boomers begin entering the program.

Policymakers from both political parties realize the Medicare population is changing and is becoming more demanding. Leaders across the political spectrum have proposed expanding the Medicare program to include a prescription drug benefit and cover more types of preventive care. However, before deciding *how* to reform the Medicare program, individuals and policymakers should stop and ask *why* they should reform the program.

Would Americans Support Allowing Younger Workers to Opt Out of Medicare?

Advocates of limited government and individual liberty would suggest either repealing the program altogether or at least allowing new workers to opt out of the Medicare payroll tax system and instead plan and provide for their own health care during retirement. Younger workers support the opt-out policy, especially if Medicare isn't reformed in the near term.

In 1998, Third Millennium board members told the National Bipartisan Medicare Commission that young Americans do not think Medicare is going to survive until their old age. The board members pointed out:

> As you probably know, Third Millennium is famous for its 1994 national survey that found more young adults believe UFOs exist than believe Social Security will exist by the time they retire. Well, you may not know that we commissioned another survey in September 1996 and asked our peers about Medicare. What did we find? A majority of them, 53% of Americans ages 18 to 34, think the TV soap opera "General Hospital" will outlast the Medicare system! In fact, a majority of Americans up to age 55 believe this.[3]

The poll was conducted by Frank Luntz, a Republican pollster, in conjunction with Democratic consultant Mark Siegel. They found that 59 percent of Americans ages 18 to 34 say that if given the choice, they would opt out of Medicare entirely and save on their own for their medical needs in old age. Luntz and Siegel stressed that, "When a majority of Generation Xers believe 'General Hospital' will outlive Medicare, you have a crisis."[4]

The opt-out approach would ensure true privatization of health care during retirement. Any policy that forces American taxpayers and seniors to participate in a government-financed program isn't a truly private health care program. The bottom line is he who pays the piper calls the tune. In other words, as long as government is financing seniors' health care, it will continue to have enormous control over individuals' personal health care decisions. Repealing Medicare, however, would raise the obvious question: What about the promises that were made to current seniors who rely on Medicare and those nearing retirement who haven't had an incentive to save for their old-age health care because they were planning on Medicare? These issues could be handled by phasing in a privatization savings plan for younger workers (as later discussed) while continuing to pay for current seniors.

There is no doubt that Medicare has become a popular program among seniors. Today many politicians run their campaigns on Medicare promises. For example, both Al Gore and George W. Bush promised Americans that if elected they would create a new prescription drug program under Medicare. With this strong political momentum, how can Americans prevent the federal government from taking control of important health care sectors, like the prescription drug market? How can younger workers make sure that they have the ability to save independently for private health care during retirement? And how can those Americans who are interested in liberty and freedom break the Medicare chains that bind them without forcing others to give up their favorite government program?

Should We Create a Universal Medicare Drug Program or Keep Government out of Seniors' Medicine Cabinets?

Reading the sensational headlines about the lack of prescription drug coverage among seniors, many may not realize that Medicare currently covers seniors' prescription drugs if they are hospitalized

Figure 6-1
SOURCES OF DRUG COVERAGE FOR MEDICARE BENEFICIARIES, 1998

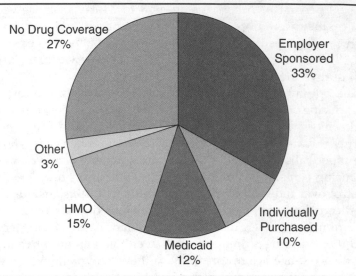

SOURCE: HCFA/Office of Strategic Planning, April 20, 2001; data are from the Medicare Current Beneficiary Survey.

and also if the drugs are prescribed as part of some limited outpatient services, such as cancer treatments. However, Medicare clearly doesn't cover most outpatient prescription drugs.[5] About 7 out of 10 Medicare beneficiaries do have coverage through employer-sponsored plans, individually purchased coverage, Medicaid, or other programs (see Figure 6-1).[6]

Seniors clearly pay more for prescription drugs because they use them more. In 1995, average prescription drug spending was $600 for noninstitutionalized Medicare beneficiaries, compared with approximately $140 for nonelderly persons.[7] The Congressional Budget Office projects outpatient drug spending will cost (regardless of payer) $1,989 per Medicare beneficiary in 2002 and $4,818 in 2011.[8]

Although more than two-thirds of seniors already have some prescription drug coverage, many are concerned that their coverage won't be adequate in coming years because prescription drug costs are increasing much faster than overall inflation. The Employee

Benefit Research Institute reported in May 1999 that prescription drug costs among private health insurers increased 17.7 percent in 1997, compared with a 4 percent or less annual growth rate for overall medical costs.[9] In 1999, spending on prescription drugs rose 16.9 percent, to $100 billion.[10]

One reason for the spending hikes has been a significant increase in the number of new drugs in the United States.[11] The number of new drugs grew from an average of 13.7 per year in the 1960s to 25.6 in the first half of the 1990s.[12] Given the pharmaceutical industry's plans to increase spending on research and development and the bipartisan support to double the federal budget for the National Institutes of Health over the coming years, one can expect further medical breakthroughs, including drugs and treatments produced by using genetic engineering and other innovative technologies. Newer drugs will cost more and they are likely to be used more frequently. Other factors that have led to higher drug costs include pharmaceutical companies marketing directly to consumers and the overall aging population. Because many patients don't pay directly for prescription drugs, they demand more than if they were directly paying the bills.

In its June 2000 report to Congress, the Medicare Payment Advisory Commission (MedPac) noted that in 1968, 87 percent of outpatient prescription drugs were paid for out of pocket. However, that share of outpatient drug spending declined to 28 percent in 1998 (see Figure 6-2). MedPac concluded, "This decline in patient liability for prescription drug costs has been one of several factors that have contributed to a 200 percent increase in total drug spending per person in the same time period."[13]

Over the years, Congress has attempted several times to add a comprehensive prescription drug benefit under Part B to cover all seniors. The attempts have failed primarily because of the expected costs of such a program. Today it is estimated that a moderately comprehensive prescription drug program would cost $1.3 trillion over the period 2001 through 2010 (see Table 6-1).[14]

Given recent forecasts for overall federal budget surpluses, politicians are likely to push for a new prescription drug benefit program under Medicare. Indeed, President Bush promised such a program during his presidential campaign. In January 2001, President Bush unveiled an "Immediate Helping Hand" (IHH) program for Medicare prescription drug coverage. The plan provides for immediate

Figure 6-2
PERCENTAGE PAID OUT OF POCKET FOR PRESCRIPTION DRUGS

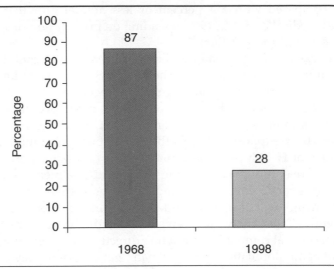

SOURCE: Medicare Payment Advisory Commission, "Medicare Beneficiaries and Prescription Drug Coverage," *Report to Congress: Selected Medicare Issues,* June 2000, p. 7.

100 percent federal funding to states to help them provide interim prescription drug coverage for seniors who need assistance paying for medications. States would have the flexibility to choose to establish or enhance drug coverage for beneficiaries. The initial Bush plan would provide prescription drug coverage for as many as 9.5 million Medicare beneficiaries. The program was estimated to cost $3 billion in fiscal year 2001 for immediate assistance to states; and then $153 billion during the period 2002–2011 as a more comprehensive program is established.[15] However, CBO estimates for prescription drug spending per Medicare beneficiary far exceed the amount budgeted per beneficiary under President Bush's IHH plan.[16]

In July 2001, President Bush announced his framework for reforming Medicare, which includes eight principles for reform. His first principle stated, "All seniors should have the option of a subsidized drug benefit as part of modernized Medicare."[17] He proposed a voluntary pharmacy discount card for seniors to purchase prescription drugs. The plan would rely on companies that manage pharmaceutical benefits to negotiate reduced prices with pharmaceutical

Table 6-1
PROJECTIONS OF PRESCRIPTION DRUG SPENDING, 2001–2010
(billions of dollars)

Calendar Year	Projected Spending
2001	$ 71
2002	81
2003	92
2004	104
2005	117
2006	131
2007	148
2008	165
2009	185
2010	205
Total	**$1,299**

SOURCE: Dan L. Crippen, "Laying the Groundwork for a Medicare Prescription Drug Benefit," Testimony before the U.S. House of Representatives, Committee on Ways and Means, Subcommittee on Health, March 27, 2001.
NOTE: January 2001 estimates.

manufacturers and to pass on the discounts to seniors.[18] Bush administration officials pointed out that the program could be established without congressional approval, thereby ensuring its implementation.

Regardless of whether this or another prescription drug program is adopted during the next year or so, American taxpayers and current and future Medicare beneficiaries should consider carefully how a new benefit program—especially a universal one—will affect their prices and choices for medicines in the coming years. Considering the government's track record for estimating Medicare costs, it is likely that a new drug-benefit program would actually cost much more in years to come than originally projected. Also, if seniors are offered prescription drug coverage under Medicare (in addition to the pharmacy discount card), employers that currently offer drug coverage to their retirees will have an incentive to drop it.

Rather than create a new federal program that could encourage employers to drop existing prescription drug coverage for retirees and lead to escalating costs in future years, President Bush should instead encourage seniors to purchase their own prescription drug coverage through a competitive private market for catastrophic health insurance and an improved Medicare + Choice program. Seniors could use the purchasing power of private insurers and pharmaceutical benefits managers to receive reduced drug prices. That would be preferable to having the federal government manage or administer a pharmacy discount program. Once the federal government gets its foot in the door, it will be difficult to prevent it from enforcing price controls and other anticompetitive policies that could eventually restrict seniors' access to the medicines of their choice.

Encouraging seniors to purchase private catastrophic insurance would not only make them more cost conscious and help control costs, it would also give seniors more control over their health care choices. Placing more money in government hands would do just the opposite: create a system whereby government officials—whether federal or state—soon would be forced to ration seniors' health care benefits because of limited funds.

Who Should Evaluate the Costs and Benefits of New Technology?

Many are excited by medical innovations that promise to extend life or improve quality of life. Seniors are going to have access to a wider array of new drugs and technologies. With increased direct marketing through television commercials, today's seniors are going to demand many new drugs, including lifestyle drugs such as Viagra. At the same time, there will be fewer workers to pay for new drugs and technologies available to the increasing number of Medicare beneficiaries.

How much can we afford for new drugs and other medical technologies? Federal Reserve Chairman Alan Greenspan touched on that issue while testifying before the National Bipartisan Commission on the Future of Medicare:

> Perhaps the hardest issue with which you [the Medicare Commission] will have to grapple is the very real possibility that the projected demands by Medicare recipients exceed a realistic estimate of our budgetary capabilities. Medical rationing is anathema to the American psyche, though it often appears in subtle forms. We know, for example, that we can never offer *all* new technologies or medical procedures immediately to *all* patients who would benefit.[19]

Until the important issue of rationing is addressed, it would be irresponsible to make another attempt to add an open-ended prescription drug entitlement to Medicare. The federal government's involvement in prescription drug coverage could have serious unintended consequences. Price controls inherent in a government-controlled plan would likely reduce pharmaceutical companies' incentives to research and produce new medicines. Instead of creating a new federal entitlement program, policymakers should consider other market-oriented approaches to Medicare reform, including tax deductions for health care, medical savings accounts, and community- or state-based programs that could serve as a safety net for the low-income elderly.

Will "Managed Competition" Work?

One of the major proposals currently being considered for reforming Medicare is to apply a managed-competition model, called "Premium Support," based on the Federal Employees Health Benefits Program (FEHBP).[20] Participants choose from a range of health plans, including fee-for-service and managed-care plans. The federal program is administered by the Office of Personnel Management, which contracts with a number of health insurance plans to provide coverage to federal employees.[21]

Proponents argue that the Premium Support proposal would provide seniors an array of choices and additional coverage for prescription drugs. It would certainly provide a steppingstone approach for moving toward a system in which seniors become accustomed to picking their own health plans. Rather than relying on a set of defined benefits, seniors would rely on a set of defined contributions. Seniors would be able to choose from a number of federally approved plans. A 2001 Kaiser Foundation/Harvard School of Public Health survey shows that some 63 percent of Americans favor giving seniors a fixed amount and allowing them to choose among private health plans, even if this policy results in higher spending (see Figure 6-3).

But critics point out some shortcomings. For example, the *New Republic* has noted that the Premium Support model supported by many of today's Republicans is just a different label for the "managed competition" proposed by Hillary Clinton in 1993.[22] Moreover, the Premium Support model still doesn't give younger workers the

Figure 6-3
AMERICANS FAVOR MEDICARE CHOICES EVEN IF COSTS RISE

"Would you still favor giving retirees this choice (of either staying in the traditional Medicare program or choosing from a list of private plans and HMOs [Health Maintenance Organizations] having different benefits and premiums, with the government paying a fixed amount toward the cost of the plan) if the traditional Medicare coverage would cost more for those who choose it than it does today?"

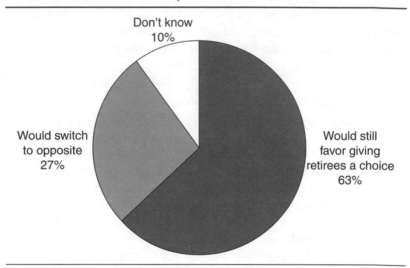

SOURCE: Survey by Henry J. Kaiser Family Foundation/Harvard School of Public Health, January 25, 2001, conducted by Princeton Survey Research Associates, November 13 through December 13, 2000, and based on telephone interviews with a national adult sample of 1,415.

ability to opt out of the Medicare program altogether, nor does it create an incentive for younger workers to save for the future costs of their private health insurance and health care services during retirement. The federal government still might limit the number of plans from which seniors can choose. Until seniors are actually paying the bills, not just picking plans, they won't have an incentive to become truly cost-conscious. Rather, they will continue to demand the highest-priced medical technologies and drugs available.

Should the Medicare Eligibility Age Be Raised?

Some have suggested raising the eligibility age as a way to cut Medicare spending. However, this seems unfair to those who have already paid higher taxes all their working lives. (There is no cap on the current 2.9 percent Medicare payroll tax.) Why should they have to pay even more when they retire? Under the current system, those who have paid substantially more in Medicare taxes receive the same medical benefits as every other Medicare beneficiary. They shouldn't be forced to pay even more for less when they retire. Moreover, raising the eligibility age won't reduce the many economic inefficiencies involved with Medicare.

How to Reform Medicare

No single organization or individual has proposed a perfect solution for transitioning Americans from the current Medicare system, in which very few seniors have true insurance, to a system that encourages individuals to purchase and maintain the private insurance they need during their entire lives, including retirement. Until individuals are back in the driver's seat, we can count on high health care costs for years to come.

It's time the nation considers reforming Medicare to encourage all Americans to become cost-conscious health care consumers and secure for themselves real coverage for catastrophic illness. A list of seven questions that every American should ask about Medicare reform proposals is shown in Box 6-1.

Medicare is a trap that forces all citizens into a dysfunctional scheme for paying health care bills. The program lacks protection for catastrophic illness. Medicare beneficiaries don't have the freedom to spend their contributions as they wish, and they certainly don't have a choice of covered benefits. How do we individualize the program to give taxpayers control over their contributions and encourage them to purchase real insurance?

Andrew Rettenmaier and Thomas Saving, economists at Texas A&M University, have developed a proposal that would transition the current pay-as-you-go Medicare system to one that relies on fully funded accounts owned by individuals.[24] Their plan for reforming Medicare includes the following:

- Workers could deposit a portion of their Medicare contributions into a personal savings account managed by a private investment company—not the U.S. Treasury.
- Workers could use their privately held accounts to purchase health insurance during retirement.

- Funds not used for health insurance could be deposited into individual medical savings accounts to pay for routine health care bills and services not covered by ordinary health insurance.

Rettenmaier and Saving point out that if younger workers set aside only $600 a year today (about half of what the average worker

---

Box 6-1
Seven Questions Every American Should Ask about Proposed Medicare Reform Proposals

1. Does the proposal place the decision of selecting health insurance plans and prescription drug coverage in the hands of seniors?

2. Does the proposal allow seniors to *sign contracts* with the health insurance plans and doctors of their choice? (If the federal government signs the contracts, it will ultimately control the important decisions, such as what treatments will be covered.)

3. Does the proposal offer seniors real health insurance coverage for catastrophic illness in which insurance companies assume financial risks? (Currently, Medicare does not cap the amount seniors must pay for catastrophic illnesses.)

4. Does the proposal encourage younger Americans to set aside funds for their long-term health care needs? (The best way to encourage this is to permit all Americans to open individual medical savings accounts.)

5. Does the proposal allow seniors to pay cash for services and products that Medicare covers in order to maintain their medical privacy?

6. Does the proposal deter Medicare fraud and abuse? Does the reform proposal rely on a government agency or individuals to control and monitor citizens' own health care dollars?

7. Does the proposal promote competition based on price *and quality* of care? (The companies chosen to process Medicare fee-for-service health care claims don't provide true insurance coverage, and they don't necessarily have to bid competitively for government contracts.[23])

will pay in Medicare taxes, including Part B, under the current system), by age 65 those deposits would grow to more than $90,000 ($180,000 for a couple) in today's dollars.[25] That is more than enough to purchase the type of health coverage currently provided by Medicare. Under their plan, those with low earnings would receive government assistance, as they do today under Medicaid. The major difference is that the subsidies would go into individual savings accounts instead of going directly to health care providers and organizations.

The Rettenmaier and Saving proposal would provide a means by which seniors could protect themselves against catastrophic costs. Insurance companies would assume true financial risks rather than just process Medicare claims. Moreover, seniors would have real assets to depend on during retirement. The proposal would encourage Americans to become cost-conscious, provide true freedom of choice, and stimulate competition in the health care industry—something that has been lacking in the Medicare program since its inception.

In addition to this particular proposal, the following principles will help individuals and policymakers determine whether a particular option will truly help restore individuals' control over their tax dollars and provide them with real insurance during their golden years:

- *Restore true choice in health care:* When enacting Medicare in 1965, President Johnson promised that nothing in the Medicare law would interfere with seniors' freedom to choose their health care, including insurance. However, over the years the Medicare program—with its more than 130,000 pages of regulations— has significantly interfered in the doctor-patient relationship. Any new Medicare reform should enable seniors to sign private contracts with health insurance plans and doctors of their choice. As long as the federal government continues signing the health insurance contracts, it will ultimately control the important health care decisions of seniors, such as what is considered "medically necessary" care under Medicare.
- *Provide insurance coverage for catastrophic illness:* Currently, Medicare does not cap the amount seniors must pay for lengthy hospital stays and expensive outpatient services. Many

MEDICARE'S MIDLIFE CRISIS

seniors—but not all—buy private Medigap insurance to cover the gaps. Instead of forcing seniors to buy additional private insurance coverage to fill Medicare's gaps, a reformed program should begin with health insurance protection for catastrophic illness that covers the large expenses seniors are least able to pay. It also should encourage seniors to pay out of pocket for less costly medical services. These sound insurance principles are the opposite of how Medicare currently works.

- *Encourage private savings:* In evaluating a Medicare reform proposal, Americans should ask, "Does the policy encourage younger Americans to set aside funds for their long-term health care needs?" The best way to encourage this is to permit all Americans to open individual medical savings accounts.

- *Promote medical privacy:* Perverse tax incentives and other regulations have encouraged Americans to rely on third parties to pay for most of their health care, including many routine services. However, individuals are becoming ever more concerned about invasions of medical privacy. Some are even opting to pay cash to maintain their privacy. Any new Medicare reform should make sure that seniors are free to pay cash for services that Medicare covers. They must be able to enter into private contracts with doctors and other health care providers without paying a penalty. The only way seniors will have true medical confidentiality is if third parties are not permitted to review their medical claims.

- *Stimulate competition based on price and quality of care:* Any new Medicare reform proposal should promote competition based on price and quality of care. In the traditional Medicare fee-for-service program, the insurance companies chosen to process claims don't necessarily have to bid competitively for government contracts.[26] They also do not assume the financial risks of beneficiaries—unlike other private insurance companies. Thus they do not have strong incentives to monitor quality of care. Allowing individuals to control more of their own money and encouraging them to purchase private health insurance covering catastrophic illness would help reduce these problems.

Will President Bush and the 107th Congress consider these important principles for Medicare reform that would help give seniors more choice of high-quality health care? After 35 years, Medicare has still not met its initial purported goal of reducing seniors' out-of-pocket health care costs. Medicare has reached a midlife crisis and needs major overhauling, not just tinkering around the edges. Instead of continuing to pour more federal dollars into a broken system, we need to consider new, innovative approaches to reforming Medicare, such as the one proposed by economists Rettenmaier and Saving.

Conclusion

For years, budget experts have been warning about the looming Medicare financial crisis. While short-term measures have helped to slow the rate of growth over the past few years, long-term projections show serious shortfalls in the coming decades. The number of seniors entering Medicare is going to grow rapidly beginning in 2011. Health care costs will also continue to rise. A new technical review panel warned the Medicare trustees that health care costs are expected to grow faster than previously projected. The present value of future additional resources needed to fund the hospital portion (Part A) alone over the next 75 years increased from $2.6 trillion in 2000 to $4.6 trillion in 2001.[27] This doesn't include Medicare Part B expenditures, which are growing faster than Part A spending.

With Medicare requiring $645 billion in general revenue subsidies during the next 10 years, policymakers are going to be forced to deal with Medicare's midlife crisis. This book explains how we got to this critical point and provides important historical lessons, in hopes that we won't repeat past mistakes. This is especially important as we consider adding a new prescription drug benefit to Medicare. Without meaningful Medicare reform first, seniors will likely face fewer choices and higher prices for prescription drugs in the coming years.

Leading financial experts warn that if the United States is going to maintain a balanced budget in the coming years, Medicare will need a major overhaul. Let's hope that the overhaul includes improvements in seniors' freedom to choose their health care— including private health insurance in lieu of traditional Medicare. Just as Americans are free to forgo public education and pay privately for their children's schooling, they should also be free to forgo enrolling in Medicare Part A when they turn age 65, and instead

97

pay privately for their health care. The current Medicare mandatory enrollment policy gives the federal government the final say on hospital and doctor fees, and it effectively prevents seniors from contracting privately with the doctors of their choice. The bottom line is that Americans should not be forced into a single-payer government health care system—Medicare—that limits their health care options and prevents them from spending money on the treatments of their choice. There is no issue more personal than one's health, especially during the golden years.

APPENDIX A Coverage under Medicare Part A: Year 2001*	
Medicare (Part A) Helps Pay For:	**Seniors Pay:**
Hospital Stays: Semiprivate room, meals, general nursing, and other hospital services and supplies. This does not include private duty nursing, a television or telephone in your room, or a private room, unless medically necessary. Inpatient mental health care coverage in a psychiatric facility is limited to 190 days in a lifetime.	**For each benefit period seniors pay:** • A total of $792 for a hospital stay of 1–60 days. • $198 per day for days 61–90 of a hospital stay. • $396 per day for days 91–150 of a hospital stay. • All costs for each day beyond 150 days.
Skilled Nursing Facility Care:** Semiprivate room, meals, skilled nursing and rehabilitative services, and other services and supplies (after a three-day hospital stay).	**For each benefit period:** • Nothing for the first 20 days. • Up to $99 per day for days 21-100. • All costs beyond the 100th day in the benefit period.
Home Health Care:** Part-time skilled nursing care, physical therapy, occupational therapy, speech-language therapy, home health aide services, durable medical equipment (such as wheelchairs, hospital beds, oxygen, and walkers) and supplies, and other services.	• Nothing for home health care services. • 20 percent of the Medicare-approved amount for durable medical equipment.
Hospice Care:** Medical and support services from a Medicare-approved hospice; drugs for symptom control and pain relief, short-term respite care, care in a hospice facility, hospital, or nursing home when necessary, and other services not otherwise covered by Medicare. Home care is also covered.	A copayment of up to $5 for outpatient prescription drugs and 5 percent of the Medicare-approved payment amount for inpatient respite care (short-term care given to a hospice patient by another caregiver so that the usual caregiver can rest). The amount seniors pay for respite care can change each year.

(continued next page)

(continued)

Blood: Pints of blood given at a hospital or skilled nursing facility during a covered stay.	For the first 3 pints of blood, unless the senior or someone else donates blood to replace what the senior used.

SOURCE: Health Care Financing Administration, U.S. Department of Health and Human Services, *Medicare and You 2001*, Publication HCFA-10050, January 2001.

* New Medicare Part A amounts will be available by January 1, 2002.

** Seniors must meet certain conditions in order for Medicare to cover these services.

Appendix B
Coverage under Medicare Part B:
Year 2001*

Medicare (Part B) Helps Pay For:	Seniors Pay:
Medical and Other Services: Doctors' services (except for routine physical exams), outpatient medical and surgical services and supplies, diagnostic tests, ambulatory surgery center facility fees for approved procedures, and durable medical equipment (such as wheelchairs, hospital beds, oxygen, and walkers). Also covers second surgical opinions, outpatient physical and occupational therapy (including speech-language therapy), and mental health services.	• $100 deductible (once per calendar year). • 20 percent of the Medicare-approved amount after the deductible, except in the outpatient setting. • 20 percent for all outpatient physical, occupational, and speech-language therapy services. • 50 percent for outpatient mental health care. • Higher amounts if the doctor does not accept Medicare fees.**
Clinical Laboratory Service: Blood tests, urinalysis, and more.	Nothing for Medicare-approved clinical laboratory services.
Home Health Care:*** Part-time skilled care, home health aide services, durable medical equipment when supplied by a home health agency while the patient receives Medicare-covered home health care, and other supplies and services.	• Nothing for Medicare-approved home health care services. • 20 percent of the Medicare-approved amount for durable medical equipment.
Outpatient Hospital Services: Services for the diagnosis or treatment of an illness or injury.	A coinsurance or fixed co-payment amount that may vary according to service.

(continued next page)

101

(continued)

Blood: Pints of blood needed as an outpatient, or as part of a Part B covered service.	For the first three pints of blood, then 20 percent of the Medicare-approved amount for additional pints of blood (after the deductible), unless the senior or someone else donates blood to replace what the senior used.
Medicare Part B also helps pay for: Ambulance services (limited coverage); artificial limbs and eyes; braces (arm, leg, back, and neck); chiropractic services (limited); emergency care; eyeglasses (one pair after cataract surgery with an intraocular lens); kidney dialysis and kidney transplants; medical supplies (items such as ostomy bags, surgical dressings, splints, casts, and some diabetic supplies); outpatient prescription drugs (very limited); preventive services (very limited types); prosthetic devices (including breast prosthesis after mastectomy); services of practitioners such as clinical psychologists, social workers, and nurse practitioners; transplants (heart, lung, kidney, pancreas, and liver) under certain conditions; and X-rays and some other diagnostic tests.	

SOURCE: Health Care Financing Administration, U.S. Department of Health and Human Services, *Medicare and You 2001*, Publication HCFA-10050, January 2001.

* New Medicare Part B amounts will be available by January 1, 2002.

** Actual amounts seniors must pay may be higher if the doctor or supplier does not accept Medicare fees.

*** Seniors must meet certain conditions in order for Medicare to cover such services or equipment.

| APPENDIX C |
What Medicare's Fee-for-Service Program *Doesn't* Cover
• Any treatment Medicare doesn't consider "medically necessary"
• Alternative medicine, including acupuncture and naturopathy (some limited chiropractic services are covered under restricted conditions)
• Most drugs and procedures not approved by the Food and Drug Administration
• Long-term care (custodial care such as assistance with eating and bathing)
• Most outpatient prescription drugs
• Most preventive services
• Routine or yearly physical exams, including vision and hearing examinations
• Health services seniors obtain while traveling outside of the United States (except under limited circumstances)

SOURCE: Health Care Financing Administration, U.S. Department of Health and Human Services, *Medicare and You 2001*, Publication HCFA-10050, January 2001.

Notes

Preface

1. President Bush's 10-year budget plan estimates a $645 billion total Medicare "deficit" between 2002 and 2011. This figure includes spending for both Medicare Part A and Part B. *A Blueprint for New Beginnings: A Responsible Budget for America's Priorities* (Washington: Government Printing Office, 2001), pp. 13–14. Until recently, Medicare spending projections did not routinely combine both parts of Medicare. Today, however, budget experts stress the importance of examining both parts of the Medicare program in projecting expenditures. The General Accounting Office recently noted, "Measurement of Medicare's sustainability can no longer be merely the traditional measure of HI [hospital insurance] Trust Fund solvency that has been used to assess the program's financial status. Both Part A expenditures financed through its Trust Fund and Part B Supplementary Medical Insurance (SMI) expenditures financed through general revenues and beneficiary premiums must be taken into consideration." See General Accounting Office, "Medicare: Higher Expected Spending and Call for New Benefit Underscore Need for Meaningful Reform," Statement of David M. Walker, Testimony before the U.S. Senate Finance Committee (107-1), GAO-01-539T, March 22, 2001.

2. The Kaiser Family Foundation/Harvard School of Public Health, *National Survey on Medicare: The Next Big Health Policy Debate?* (Menlo Park, Calif.: Kaiser Family Foundation, 1998), p. 7.

Chapter 1

1. The name has been changed in deference to a request for privacy. The information is based on documented evidence, including a copy of an application form "Application for Retirement Insurance Benefits," processed by a Social Security office and correspondence from the Office of the General Counsel, Health Care Financing Administration, U.S. Department of Health and Human Services.

2. U.S. Senate Committee on Finance (106-2), Statement of Robert R. Waller, M.D., President Emeritus, Mayo Foundation, Chairman, The Healthcare Leadership Council, on behalf of The Healthcare Leadership Council, February 24, 2000.

3. 42 C.F.R 406.6 and 20 C.F.R 404.640.

4. The term "private contracting" is often used to describe Medicare beneficiaries' ability to pay privately for medical services. The restrictive rule on private contracting under Medicare does not apply to services that Medicare does *not* cover, such as most outpatient prescription drugs.

5. John S. Hoff, *Medicare Private Contracting* (Washington: AEI Press, 1998); *United Seniors Association, Inc., et al. v. Shalala*, 182 F.3d 965 (D.C. Cir. 1999).

6. Health Care Financing Administration (HCFA) and Office of Strategic Planning, U.S. Department of Health and Human Services, *Excerpts from A Profile of Medicare Chartbook: 1998*, 1998, p. 3; *Laying the Groundwork for a Medicare Prescription Drug Benefit*, U.S. House Ways and Means Committee (107-1), Subcommittee on Health, Testimony of Dan L. Crippen, Congressional Budget Office, March 27, 2001.

7. Medicare covered 39 million people during 2000 (34 million aged and 5 million disabled beneficiaries). See Board of Trustees, Federal Hospital Insurance Trust Fund, *2001 Annual Report of the Board of Trustees of the Federal Hospital Insurance Trust Fund*, March 19, 2001, p. 4.

8. Part A totaled $131.1 billion. Part B totaled $90.7 billion. See ibid; Crippen.

9. Henry J. Kaiser Family Foundation, "Medicaid's Role for Low-Income Medicare Beneficiaries," *Kaiser Commission on Medicaid and the Uninsured: Key Facts*, February 2001.

10. According to U.S. Department of Health and Human Services Inspector General June Gibbs Brown, the Health Care Financing Administration—the agency that administers Medicare and Medicaid—is the largest single purchaser of health care in the world. U.S. Senate Appropriations Committee (106-2), Subcommittee on Labor, Health and Human Services, Education: Testimony of June Gibbs Brown, *Medicare Waste, Fraud & Abuse*, March 9, 2000.

11. For an overview of Medicare coverage, see the HCFA annual handbook for beneficiaries. The most recent handbook is *Medicare & You 2001*, HCFA-10050, January 2001, p. 6.

12. HCFA and Office of Strategic Planning, U.S. Department of Health and Human Services, p. 4.

13. Board of Trustees, Hospital Insurance (HI) Trust Fund, *2001 Annual Report*, p. 5.

14. Board of Trustees, Supplementary Medical Insurance Trust Fund (SMI), *2001 Annual Report*, p. 5.

15. HCFA, *Health Care Financing Review: Medicare and Medicaid Statistical Supplement, 1999*, Publication 03417, November 1999, p. 5.

16. Waller.

17. Henry J. Kaiser Family Foundation, "Medicare Managed Care," *The Medicare Program*, February 2001.

18. Greg Scandlen, "Medicare Reform," *Patient Power Report*, August 1997, p. 4.

19. Note: Only 14 percent of seniors living in rural areas have a Medicare + Choice option. Medicare HMO enrollment is concentrated in a few states, predominantly California (26%), Florida (12%), Pennsylvania (9%), New York (7%), Ohio (4%), Arizona (4%), and Massachusetts (4%). Henry J. Kaiser Family Foundation, "Medicare Managed Care," *The Medicare Program*.

20. Bruce Merlin Fried and Janice Ziegler, *The Medicare + Choice Program: Is It Code Blue?* (Washington: ShawPittman, June 8, 2000), p. 5.

21. Marsha Gold, "Medicare + Choice: An Interim Report Card," *Health Affairs* 20, no. 4 (July/August 2001), p. 121.

22. HCFA, *Medicare & You 2001*, pp. 6, 71.

23. Ibid., p. 6.

24. Robert Moffit, "Medicare Medicine," *Washington Times*, June 1, 1999, p. A15.

25. HCFA, *Medicare & You 2001*, pp. 6, 63–64.

26. *Helvering v. Davis*, 301 U.S. 619 (1937) and *Flemming v. Nestor*, 363 U.S. 603 (1960).

27. Charles E. Rounds, Jr., "Property Rights: The Hidden Issue of Social Security Reform," the Cato Project on Social Security Privatization, SSP No. 19, April 19, 2000,

pp. 2–5. See also Peter J. Ferrara and Michael D. Tanner, *Common Cents Common Dreams: A Layman's Guide to Social Security Privatization* (Washington: Cato Institute, 1998), pp. 18–19.

28. When seniors obtain services under traditional Medicare, their Medicare-participating providers bill the contractors that process claims for Medicare, and payment is sent directly to providers. Seniors receive an "Explanation of Medicare Benefits" or a "Medicare Summary Notice." However, if a doctor does *not* take Medicare assignment (agrees with Medicare to accept the Medicare-approved amount as full payment), seniors are responsible for paying the full amount, even though the doctor must submit the bill (there is a limit on the amount a doctor can bill). Medicare will reimburse seniors later for its share of the bill. Approximately 96 percent of Medicare claims involve no balance billing. HCFA, *Medicare & You 2001*, p. 56; Physician Payment Review Commission, *Annual Report to Congress*, 1997, pp. 313, 314.

29. Sylvia Law, *Blue Cross: What Went Wrong?* (New Haven: Yale University Press, 1976), p. 8, cited in Lawrence D. Weiss, *No Benefit: Crisis in America's Health Insurance Industry* (Boulder, Colo.: Westview Press, 1992), p. 11. See also U.S. House of Representatives Committee on Ways and Means, *National Health Insurance Resource Book* (Washington: Government Printing Office, April 1974), p. 220.

30. Jeffrey C. Bauer, *Not What the Doctor Ordered: Reinventing Medical Care in America* (Chicago: Probus Publishing Company, 1994), p. 42.

31. U.S. Senate Committee on Finance (106-1), Mary Nell Lehnhard, Testimony of the Blue Cross and Blue Shield Association on Medicare Reform, May 27, 1999.

32. Although Medicare automatically enrolls most seniors in the program when they reach age 65, Medicare may function as the secondary payer in some limited circumstances. The HCFA asserts that federal law (Medicare) takes precedence over state law and private contracts; thus, for certain categories of people (such as employed seniors with group health insurance covering 20 or more workers), Medicare may be the secondary payer regardless of state law or employer plan provisions. The federal requirements are found in Section 1862(b) of the Social Security Act, 42 U.S.C. Section 1395y(b)(5); applicable regulations are found at 42 C.F.R. Part 411 (1990); HCFA, 2001.

33. Jennifer O'Sullivan, "Medicare Catastrophic Coverage Act of 1988 (P.L. 100-360)," *CRS Report for Congress*, Congressional Research Service, Report 89-155 EPW, March 3, 1989, p. CRS-2. The Social Security Administration's Operation Manual includes a policy titled "Waiver of HI [Hospital Insurance] Entitlement by Monthly Beneficiary," which reads as follows: "A. INTRODUCTION: Some individuals entitled to monthly benefits have asked to waive their HI entitlement because of religious or philosophical reasons or because they prefer other health insurance. B. POLICY: Individuals entitled to monthly benefits, which confer eligibility for HI may not waive HI entitlement. The only way to avoid HI entitlement is through withdrawal of the monthly benefit application. Withdrawal requires repayment of all RSDI [Retirement, Survivors and Disability Insurance] and HI benefit payments made." Social Security Operation Manual, Policy no. HI 00801.002; personal telephone communication with Marty Zemel, Social Security Administration, May 20, 1998.

34. Kenneth M. Morris, Alan M. Siegel, and Virginia B. Morris, *The Wall Street Journal Guide to Planning Your Financial Future* (New York: Lightbulb Press, Inc., and Dow Jones & Co., Inc., 1995), p. 155.

35. Jennifer O'Sullivan, Celinda Franco, Beth Fuchs, and Richard Price, "Medicare: FY1998 Budget," *CRS Report for Congress*, Congressional Research Service, Report 97-288 EPW, April 15, 1997, p. CRS-17.

36. Edward R. Annis, M.D., "History Lesson," *Frontline Newsletter*, June 1996.

37. Affidavit of J. Patrick Rooney, filed in the United States District Court for the District of Columbia, on behalf of *United Seniors Association, Inc., et al. v. Shalala*. The affidavit was sworn and subscribed on December 26, 1997.

38. Crippen.

39. Steve Teske, *BNA's Health Care Policy Report* (Washington: Bureau of National Affairs, July 2, 2001), p. 1036.

40. Charles N. Kahn III, Statement of the Health Insurance Association of America on Medicare Reform, Testimony before the U.S. Senate Finance Committee (106-1), May 27, 1999; Samuel Morgante, Statement of the Health Insurance Association of America on the Importance of Long-Term Care Insurance in Planning the Retirement of Baby Boomers, Testimony before the U.S. Senate Special Committee on Aging (105-2), March 9, 1998, p. 4.

41. Meredith Bagby and Alden Levy, National Board Members of Third Millennium, Testimony before the National Bipartisan Commission on the Future of Medicare, April 21, 1998.

42. Technical Review Panel on the Medicare Trustees Reports, *Review of Assumptions and Methods of the Medicare Trustees' Financial Projections*, December 2000, p. 42.

43. General Accounting Office, "Medicare: Higher Expected Spending and Call for New Benefit Underscore Need for Meaningful Reform," Statement of David M. Walker, Testimony before the U.S. Senate Finance Committee (107-1), GAO-01-539T, March 22, 2001.

44. Ibid.

45. Crippen.

46. Board of Trustees, Federal Hospital Insurance Trust Fund, *2000 Annual Report of the Board of Trustees of the Federal Hospital Insurance Trust Fund*, March 30, 2000, p. 18. Between 1967 and 1997, the average annual rate of change for Medicare Part A services (all types) was 13.4 percent. However, there was wide variation in growth according to type of Medicare Part A services: inpatient hospital services increased by 12.7 percent; skilled nursing facilities services grew by 13.7 percent; and home health care services under Medicare Part A increased by 25.9 percent between 1967 and 1997. See HCFA, *Health Care Financing Review: Medicare and Medicaid Statistical Supplement 1999*, p. 109.

47. *A Blueprint for New Beginnings: A Responsible Budget for America's Priorities* (Washington: Government Printing Office, 2001), p. 13.

48. Alan Greenspan, Board of Governors of the Federal Reserve System, Testimony before the National Bipartisan Commission on the Future of Medicare, April 20, 1998, p. 14.

49. U.S. Senate Committee on the Budget (107-1), *The Budget and Economic Outlook: Fiscal Years 2002–2011*, Statement of Barry B. Anderson, Congressional Budget Office, January 31, 2001.

50. Ibid.; HI Board of Trustees, *2001 Annual Report*, pp. 15–17.

51. General Accounting Office, "Medicare: Higher Expected Spending and Call for New Benefit Underscore Need for Meaningful Reform."

52. *A Blueprint for New Beginnings: A Responsible Budget for America's Priorities*, p. 13.

53. U.S. House Committee on Energy and Commerce, Subcommittee on Health (107-1), *Medicare Reform: Providing Prescription Drug Coverage for Seniors*, Statement of Dan L. Crippen, Congressional Budget Office, May 16, 2001.

54. Ibid.

55. HI Board of Trustees, *2001 Annual Report*, pp. 2–3.

56. The average annual rate of change for Medicare Part B was 14.3 percent between 1967 and 1997. See HCFA, *Health Care Financing Review: Medicare and Medicaid Statistical Supplement, 1999*, p. 109.

57. SMI Board of Trustees, *2001 Annual Report*, p. 2.

58. *A Blueprint for New Beginnings: A Responsible Budget for America's Priorities*, p. 13.

59. U.S. Senate Finance Committee (106-1), Statement of Charles N. Kahn III, the Health Insurance Association of America, on Medicare Reform, May 27, 1999; Testimony before the U.S. Senate Special Committee on Aging (105-2), Statement of Samuel Morgante, Health Insurance Association of America, on the Importance of Long Term Care Insurance in Planning the Retirement of Baby Boomers, March 9, 1998.

60. Marilyn Moon, *Growth in Medicare Spending: What Will Beneficiaries Pay?* (Washington: Urban Institute, May 1999), pp. 3–4.

61. Projections have been corrected to adjust for the general rate of inflation in all consumer prices; thus they can be compared with 1998 levels of spending and income. Ibid.

62. General Accounting Office, "Medicare Reform: Leading Proposals Lay Groundwork, While Design Decisions Lie Ahead," Statement of David M. Walker, Testimony before the U.S. Senate Committee on Finance (106-2), GAO/T-HEHS/AIMD-00-103, February 24, 2000, p. 2.

63. Office of Management and Budget, *The Budget for Fiscal Year 2001* (Washington: Government Printing Office, 2000), p. 253.

64. Normandy Brangan and Mary Jo Gibson, *FYI: The Cost of Prescription Drugs: Who Needs Help?* (Washington: AARP Public Policy Institute, 2000), p. 1.

65. Moon, p. 11.

66. U.S. Department of Health and Human Services, "Improper Fiscal Year 2000 Medicare Fee-for-Service Payments," Report A-17-00-02000, March 6, 2001.

67. Former Department of Health and Human Services (HHS) principal deputy general counsel Robert Charrow emphasizes that "Merely because we are constantly being told that there is a significant amount of fraud in our health care system does not mean that there is. . . . The fact that HCFA points to $12.6 billion lost due to honest errors (e.g., miscoding and the like) is a meaningless statistic. . . . Furthermore, many of the so-called errors actually involve honest differences of opinion regarding how medicine ought to be practiced—i.e., what is 'medically necessary.'" Grace Marie Arnett, Jonathan Emord, Laurence Huntoon, M.D., and Robert Charrow, "How Medicare Paperwork Abuses Doctors and Harms Patients," *Heritage Lectures*, No. 665, May 11, 2000.

68. Ibid.

69. Democratic Policy Committee, "Medicare Trustees' Report Highlights Need for Action," *DPC Special Report* (Washington: Democratic Policy Committee, 1997), Publication no. SR-09-Social Services, p. 3.

70. *U.S. Code Congressional and Administrative News*, [1960] 86-2, p. 3609.

71. U.S. Department of Health, Education, and Welfare, "Health Insurance Coverage: United States, July 1962–June 1963," Public Health Service Publication no. 1000-Series 10-No. 11, August 1964, p. 1.

72. U.S. House of Representatives, Committee on Ways and Means, *Summary of Major Provisions of the Medical Assistance for the Aged Program (Kerr-Mills Law): Public Law 86-778*, [1965] 89-1, pp. 1–4.

73. *U.S. Code Congressional and Administrative News*, [1960] 86-2, pp. 1299, 3608.

74. Ibid., p. 3609.

75. Ibid.

76. Associated Press, "Medical Aid Bill Signed by President," *Los Angeles Times,* September 14, 1960.

77. James W. Wiggins and Helmut Schoeck, "The Aging: Neither Indigent Nor Childlike: They Want Government Aid as Very Last, Not First, Resort," *Wall Street Journal,* August 18, 1960.

78. The Centers for Disease Control and Prevention's 1998 data combined "fair and poor" health. Centers for Disease Control and Prevention, National Center for Health Statistics, *Health, United States, 2000,* p. 233.

Chapter 2

1. Although Germany is often cited as the country most responsible for the political movement toward social insurance, the first compulsory health insurance *law* was enacted in the state of Prussia in 1854. See Peter A. Corning, *The Evolution of Medicare . . . from idea to law* (Washington: Government Printing Office, 1969), pp. 3–4.

2. Laurene A. Graig, *Health of Nations: An International Perspective on U.S. Health Care Reform* (Washington: CQ Press, 1999), p. 45.

3. A. Lawrence Lowell et al., *Final Report of the Commission on Medical Education* (New York: Commission on Medical Education, 1932), p. 42.

4. Ronald L. Numbers, ed., *Compulsory Health Insurance: The Continuing American Debate* (Westport, Conn.: Greenwood Press, 1982), p. ix; Lowell et al., p. 44.

5. Corning, p. 4.

6. Graig, pp. 13, 127.

7. Numbers, p. 118.

8. The Socialist Party, *Socialist National Platform* (Chicago: Socialist Party, 1904), pp. 5–6.

9. Corning, p. 6.

10. Ibid., p. 17.

11. Ibid., p. 6.

12. Ibid., pp. 8–9.

13. Richard Harris, *A Sacred Trust* (New York: The New American Library, 1966), p. 5.

14. Explanation about advocates' strategy is discussed in Numbers, p. x. See also *Helvering v. Davis,* 301 U.S. 619 (1937).

15. American Medical Association, "Proceedings of the Detroit Session: Minutes of the Sixty-Seventh Annual Session of the American Medical Association, Held at Detroit, Mich., June 12–16, 1916," *Journal of the American Medical Association* LXVI, no. 25 (1916), p. 1950.

16. Ibid.

17. Corning, p. 9.

18. Ibid.

19. Numbers, p. 6.

20. Corning, pp. 20–22.

21. Numbers, p. x.

22. Corning, p. 10.

23. Harris. The book *A Sacred Trust* chronicles the AMA's role in initially supporting compulsory health insurance, later opposing it, and then eventually helping to draw up regulations to implement Medicare.

24. Ibid., pp. 6–7.

25. The eight foundations that supported the Committee on the Costs of Medical Care were the Carnegie Corporation, the Josiah Macy, Jr. Foundation, the Milbank Memorial Fund, the New York Foundation, the Rockefeller Foundation, the Julius Rosenwald Fund, the Russell Sage Foundation, and the Twentieth Century Fund. Committee on the Costs of Medical Care, *Medical Care for the American People: The Final Report of the Committee on the Costs of Medical Care* (Washington: U.S. Department of Health, Education, and Welfare, 1970), pp. xvii–xviii.

26. Corning, p. 25.

27. Harris, p. 7.

28. Arthur J. Viseltear, "Compulsory Health Insurance and the Definition of Public Health," in Ronald L. Numbers, ed., *Compulsory Health Insurance: The Continuing American Debate* (Westport, Conn.: Greenwood Press, 1982), p. 30.

29. Ibid., p. 28.

30. Rashi Fein, *Medical Care, Medical Costs* (Cambridge, Mass.: Harvard College, 1986), pp. 10–11.

31. Committee on the Costs of Medical Care, pp. viii and xvii.

32. Ibid., p. 171.

33. Ibid., p. 9.

34. Ibid., pp. xv–xx.

35. Ibid., p. 146.

36. Ibid., p. 50.

37. Paul Starr, "Transformation in Defeat: The Changing Objectives of National Health Insurance, 1915–1980," in Ronald L. Numbers, ed. *Compulsory Health Insurance: The Continuing American Debate* (Westport, Conn.: Greenwood Press, 1982), p. 127.

38. Committee on the Costs of Medical Care, pp. 13–14.

39. The 1932 figure of $3.2 billion included both private sector and government spending on health care. See ibid., pp. 2, 14. The 1932 figure of $3.2 billion was adjusted for inflation and compared with 1999 dollars by using the Federal Reserve Bank of Minneapolis consumer price index inflation calculator, www.minneapolis fed.org/economy/calc/cpihome.html. Accessibility verified July 15, 2001.

40. In 1929, health care spending was nearly $30 per capita, which constituted approximately 4 percent of the money income in the country. See Committee on the Costs of Medical Care, p. 13. In 1998, per capita health spending was $4,094; national health expenditures as a percent of GDP totaled 13.5 percent. See Katharine Levit et al., "Health Spending in 1998: Signals of Change," *Health Affairs* 19, no. 1 (January/February 2000): 124.

41. Committee on the Costs of Medical Care, pp. 104–105.

42. Ibid., pp. 15, 26, and 137.

43. Ibid., pp. 28–29.

44. Ibid., p. 33.

45. Ibid., pp. 136, 143.

46. The CCMC published a final report and two minority reports simultaneously in 1932.

47. Committee on the Costs of Medical Care, pp. 164, 179.

48. Ibid., p. 158.

49. Ibid., pp. 155–159.

50. Ibid., p. 179.

51. Ibid., p. vii.

52. Howard S. Berliner, "The Origins of Health Insurance for the Aged," *International Journal of Health Services* 3, no. 3 (1973): 465.

53. Committee on the Costs of Medical Care, p. viii.

54. *American Medical Association v. United States,* 317 U.S. 519 (1943).

55. Harris, p. 18.

56. Ibid.

57. Ibid., p. 10.

58. In 1999, Americans spent $4,358 per capita or 15.2 percent of per capita personal income on health care services. HCFA, Office of the Actuary; U.S. Department of Commerce, Bureau of Economic Analysis, *State Personal Income, 1929–1999,* 2000; Bureau of the Census, *Historical Statistics of the United States: Colonial Times to 1970, Bicentennial Edition, Part 1* (Washington: Government Printing Office, 1975), p. 73.

59. Starr, p. 126.

60. Ibid., p. 117.

61. Committee on the Costs of Medical Care, pp. 125, 155–157.

62. Susan Feigenbaum, "'Body Shop' Economics: What's Good for Our Cars May Be Good for Our Health," *Regulation* 15, no. 4 (1992).

63. Lowell et al., pp. 47–53.

64. Ibid.; Committee on the Costs of Medical Care, pp. 155–159.

65. Lowell et al., p. 47.

66. Starr, p. 123.

67. Ibid.

68. Hadley Cantril, *The Psychology of Social Movements* (Huntington, N.Y.: Robert F. Krieger, 1941), p. 175.

69. Harris, pp. 8–9.

70. Eugene Feingold, *Medicare: Policy and Politics* (San Francisco: Chandler Publishing Company, 1966), pp. 91–92; Harris, p. 9.

71. Theodore R. Marmor, *The Politics of Medicare* (Chicago: Aldine, 1973), pp. 8–9.

72. Hadley Cantril, *Public Opinion 1935–1946* (Princeton: Princeton University Press, 1951), pp. 442–443.

73. Marmor, p. 13.

74. Ibid.

75. Howard Berliner is currently associate professor and chair, Health Services Management and Policy, Milano Graduate School of Management and Urban Policy, New School University. He formerly held many consulting positions, including the preparation and drafting of National Health Service legislation introduced in Congress in 1977 by Representative Dellums of California. See www.newschool.edu/milano/howard/CV.HTM. Accessibility verified July 14, 2001.

76. Berliner, p. 466.

77. Numbers, p. xi.

78. Harris, pp. 59–60.

79. Marmor, p. 18. Marmor notes that the statistical profiling would continue for the next 15 years. He also notes that between 1957 and 1958 seniors' medical expenses averaged $177 per year, more than double the $86 spent per person under 65. (One would expect seniors' medical expenses to be much higher. Today they spend almost three times as much as younger persons.)

80. Ibid., p. 20.

81. I. S. Falk, "Medical Care in the USA—1932–1972: Problems, Proposals and Programs from the Committee on the Costs of Medical Care to the Committee for

National Health Insurance," *The Milbank Memorial Quarterly Fund/Health and Society* 51, no. I (Winter 1973): 15.

Chapter 3

1. U.S. House of Representatives, Committee on Ways and Means (89-1), *Summary of Major Provisions of the Medical Assistance for the Aged Program (Kerr-Mills Law): Public Law 86-778*, 1965, pp. 1–4.

2. Ibid.

3. Staff reporter, "Democrats to Ask Package Financing of Care for Aged," *Wall Street Journal*, August 17, 1960, p. 3.

4. Ibid.

5. Staff reporter, "Senate Defeats Kennedy on Medical Aid to Aged as 19 Democrats Defect; He Suggests Adjournment," *Wall Street Journal*, August 24, 1960.

6. Ibid.

7. *U.S. Code Congressional and Administrative News* [1960] 86-2, p. 1299.

8. U.S. Department of Health, Education, and Welfare, *U.S. Department of Health, Education, and Welfare Annual Report* (Washington: Government Printing Office, 1961), p. iii.

9. Wilbur J. Cohen, "Reflections on the Enactment of Medicare and Medicaid," *Health Care Financing Review/1985 Annual Supplement*, 1985, p. 3.

10. U.S. Department of Health, Education, and Welfare, p. 60.

11. U.S. Senate Committee on Finance (89-1), *Social Security: Hearings* [on H.R. 6675], April–May 1965, p. 163.

12. Ibid., p. 636.

13. U.S. Department of Health, Education, and Welfare, "Health Insurance Coverage: United States, July 1962–June 1963," Public Health Service Publication no. 1000-Series 10-No. 11, August 1964.

14. U.S. Senate Committee on Finance, pp. 1127–1130.

15. U.S. Department of Health, Education and Welfare, p. 1.

16. Celinda Franco, "The Hill-Burton Program," *CRS Report for Congress*, Congressional Research Service, Report 94-88 EPW, May 2, 1997, p. CRS-1.

17. U.S. Department of Health, Education and Welfare, *HEW Annual Report: 1966* (Washington: Government Printing Office, 1966), p. 73.

18. William A. Pearman and Philip Starr, *Medicare: A Handbook on the History and Issues of Health Care Services for the Elderly* (New York: Garland Publishing, 1988), pp. 6–7.

19. Kennedy captured 49.94 percent of the popular votes compared to Nixon's 49.77 percent and defeated Nixon by only 118,574 popular votes, 0.17 percent of the 68,531,917 popular votes cast in 1960. Bureau of the Census, *Historical Statistics of the United States: Colonial Times to 1970* (Washington: Government Printing Office, 1975), p. 1073.

20. Theodore R. Marmor, *The Politics of Medicare* (Chicago: Aldine, 1973), p. 39.

21. Ibid., p. 54.

22. Memo, Lawrence F. O'Brien to the President [Johnson], January 27, 1964, Office Files of Mike Mantos, Box 9, LBJ Library.

23. Irving Bernstein, *Guns or Butter: The Presidency of Lyndon Johnson* (New York: Oxford University Press, 1996), p. 164.

24. Drew Pearson, "Cigarette Action Took 10 Years," *Washington Post*, January 11, 1964, p. D7.

25. Ibid.

26. Bernstein, p. 164.

27. American Medical Association, *1959–1968 Digest of Official Actions* (Chicago: American Medical Association, 1971), p. 375.

28. Barbara Dreyfuss, "Twenty Years Later: Key Players Reminisce," *The Internist*, March 1985, p. 9.

29. Sheri I. David, *With Dignity: The Search for Medicare and Medicaid* (Westport, Conn.: Greenwood Press, 1985), p. 124.

30. Charlotte Twight, "Medicare's Origin: The Economics and Politics of Dependency," *Cato Journal* 16, no. 3 (Winter 1997): 319.

31. Ibid., p. 326.

32. Social Security Administration, *Social Security: Facts and Figures*, SSA Publication 05-10011, May 1997, p. 1.

33. Pearman and Starr, p. 8.

34. David, p. 130.

35. Ibid., p. 129.

36. Arlen J. Large, "Mills and Medicare: How Federal Health Insurance Plan Evolved in Congress," *Wall Street Journal*, August 2, 1965.

37. Cohen, p. 6.

38. O'Brien, January 27, 1964.

39. Memo, Lawrence F. O'Brien to the President [Johnson], September 23, 1964, Legislation EX/LE/IS, Box 75, LBJ Library.

40. Transcript, Wilbur Mills Oral History Interview, March 25, 1987, by Michael L. Gillette, Interview II, tape 1, side 1, page II-3, LBJ Library.

41. Twight, p. 334.

42. Ibid., p. 333.

43. Large.

44. David, p. 131.

45. Pearman and Starr, p. 9.

46. U.S. Senate Committee on Finance, p. 818.

47. Pearman and Starr, p. 9.

48. Dreyfuss, p. 9.

49. Harris, p. 215.

50. Ibid., p. 216.

51. Social Security Administration, *A Brief History of Social Security: Social Security 60th Anniversary*, SSA Publication 21-059, July 1995, p. 13.

52. James Z. Appel, M.D., "We the People of the United States—Are We Sheep?" *Journal of the American Medical Association* 193, no. 1 (July 5, 1965): 116–117.

53. U.S. Senate Committee on Finance, p. 1203.

54. "Medicare Boycott Urged for Doctors," *New York Times*, August 5, 1965, p. 1.

55. Jonathan Spivak, "Medicare's Impact: Officials See Program Bringing General Gains in U.S. Medical Care," *Wall Street Journal*, July 30, 1965, p. 1.

56. John Colombotos, "Physicians and Medicare: A Before-After Study of the Effects of Legislation on Attitudes," *American Sociological Review* 34, no. 3 (June 1969): 318–334.

57. Howard S. Berliner, "The Origins of Health Insurance for the Aged," *International Journal of Health Services* 3, no. 3 (1973): 472.

58. Ibid., p. 471.

59. I. S. Falk, "Medical Care in the USA—1932–1972: Problems, Proposals and Programs from the Committee on the Costs of Medical Care to the Committee for National Health Insurance," *The Milbank Memorial Quarterly Fund/Health and Society* 51, no. 1 (Winter 1973): 18.

60. Twight, p. 334.

Chapter 4

1. U.S. Senate Committee on Finance (89-1), *Social Security: Hearings [on H.R. 6675],* April–May 1965, pp. 95–96.

2. Ibid.

3. Information provided by Barkev Sanders, former statistician for the Social Security Administration. U.S. Senate Committee on Finance, p. 1142.

4. U.S. Senate Committee on Finance, p. 135.

5. Ibid., p. 113.

6. Social Security Administration, "Social Security: Facts and Figures," SSA Publication 05-10011, May 1997, p. 6.

7. Social Security Administration/Internal Revenue Service, *Reporter: A Newsletter for Employers,* Winter 2000.

8. Personal communication with Roland (Guy) King, former HCFA actuary, May 29, 2000.

9. Robert J. Myers, "How Bad Were the Original Actuarial Estimates for Medicare's Hospital Insurance Program?" *The Actuary,* February 1994, p. 7.

10. HCFA, *Health Care Financing Review: Medicare and Medicaid Statistical Supplement, 1999,* p. 109.

11. U.S. Senate Committee on Finance, p. 1231.

12. HCFA, p. 106.

13. Jennifer O'Sullivan, "Medicare: Part B Premiums," *CRS Report for Congress,* Congressional Research Service, Report 96-867 EPW, October 31, 1996, p. CRS-1.

14. Board of Trustees, Federal Supplementary Medical Insurance Trust Fund, *2001 Annual Report of the Board of Trustees of the Federal Supplementary Medical Insurance Trust Fund,* March 19, 2001, pp. 4–5.

15. Jack Wooldridge, ed., "Federal Health Estimates—300% Wrong," *Nation's Business* (Washington: Chamber of Commerce of the United States, November 1964) 52, no. 11: 31–33, 112–114.

16. Ibid., p. 112.

17. Ibid., p. 33.

18. Ibid., p. 32.

19. Ibid., p. 112.

20. Ibid., p. 114.

21. John D. Morris, "President Signs Medicare Bill; Praises Truman," *New York Times,* July 31, 1965, p. 1.

22. Richard Reeves, "Hospitals' Rates Are Rising Faster than Living Costs," *New York Times,* September 6, 1966, p. 1.

23. Martin Tolchin, "Doctors' Fees Up as Much as 300% under Medicare," *New York Times,* August 19, 1966, p. 1.

24. Harold M. Schmeck Jr., "Change Foreseen in Medical Care: Conferees in Capital Agree on Need and Inevitability," *New York Times,* July 2, 1967, p. 26.

25. The Tax Foundation study is cited in "Medical Care Cost Doubles in 3 Years," *New York Times*, September 9, 1968, p. 47.

26. Special to the *New York Times*, "Excerpts from President Johnson's Message," *New York Times*, March 5, 1968, p. 22.

27. Ibid.

28. Ted Marmor and Julie Beglin, "Medicare and How It Grew . . . and Grew . . . and Grew," *Boston Globe*, May 7, 1995, p. 74.

29. The $7.9 billion 1971 figure was adjusted to 1967 dollars using the Federal Reserve Bank of Minneapolis consumer price index inflation calculator, www.minneapolisfed.org/economy/calc/cpihome.html. Accessibility verified July 15, 2001.

30. William A. Pearman and Philip Starr, *Medicare: A Handbook on the History and Issues of Health Care Services for the Elderly* (New York: Garland Publishing, 1988), p. 23.

31. Health expenditures accounted for 5.9 percent of gross national product in 1965. Bureau of the Census, *Historical Statistics of the United States: Colonial Times to 1970, Bicentennial Edition, Part 1* (Washington: Government Printing Office, 1975), p. 74.

32. The proportion of gross domestic product devoted to health care in 1999 was 13 percent; it is estimated to be 13.9 percent in 2002. Medicare spending was $213.6 billion in 1999, accounting for nearly one-sixth of total expenditures ($1,210.7 billion in 1999). Stephen Heffler et al., "Health Spending Growth Up in 1999; Faster Growth Expected in the Future," *Health Affairs* 20, no. 2 (March/April 2001): 193, 194, 197.

33. Jason S. Lee, "Quality of Care Issues in Medicare Reform," *CRS Report for Congress*, Congressional Research Service, Report 96-581 EPW, June 26, 1996.

34. Pearman and Starr, p. 17.

35. Twila Brase, "HMOs' Rise Driven by Government, Not Market," *Intellectual Ammunition*, November/December 1998.

36. Pearman and Starr, pp. 16–17.

37. Steven Hayward and Erik Peterson, "The Medicare Monster," *Reason*, January 1993, p. 24.

38. Ibid.

39. Ibid.; Health Care Financing Administration, p. 109.

40. Jennifer O'Sullivan, "Medicare: Financing the Part A Hospital Insurance Program," *CRS Report for Congress*, Congressional Research Service, Report RS20173, April 22, 1999, pp. CRS-5–CRS-6.

41. Board of Trustees, Federal Hospital Insurance Trust Fund, *1999 Annual Report of the Board of Trustees of the Federal Hospital Insurance Trust Fund,* March 30, 1999, p. 24.

42. General Accounting Office, "Medicare Fraud and Abuse: DOJ Has Improved Oversight of False Claims Act Guidance," GAO-01-506, March 2001.

Chapter 5

1. See, for example, the Democratic Policy Committee's summary of Medicare's success in "Medicare Trustees' Report Highlights: Need for Action," *DPC Special Report* (Washington: Democratic Policy Committee, April 30, 1997). The report doesn't cite the source (or year) it uses to back the claim, "For those 65 and older in the United States, life expectancy is now higher than any other country in the world, with the exception of Japan."

2. Gerard Anderson and Peter Sotir Hussey, "Comparing Health System Performance in OECD Countries," *Health Affairs* 20, no. 3 (May/June 2001): 219–232.

3. Alan Greenspan, Board of Governors of the Federal Reserve System, Testimony before the National Bipartisan Commission on the Future of Medicare, April 20, 1998, p. 6.

4. Anderson and Hussey, p. 226.

5. Greenspan, p. 6.

6. Ibid., pp. 6–7.

7. Bureau of the Census, *Historical Statistics of the United States: Colonial Times to 1970, Bicentennial Edition, Part 1* (Washington: Government Printing Office, 1975), p. 55.

8. Anderson and Hussey, pp. 219–232.

9. Robert L. Clark and Joseph F. Quinn, "The Economic Status of the Elderly," *Medicare Brief*, No. 4 (Washington: National Academy of Social Insurance, 1999), pp. 2–3.

10. Democratic Policy Committee, p. 8.

11. *Economic Report of the President* (Washington: Government Printing Office, 1964); *Older Americans 2000: Key Indicators of Well-Being* (Washington: Federal Interagency Forum on Aging Related Statistics, 2000).

12. United Press International, "Reuther Assails Medicare Billing," *New York Times*, March 23, 1967, p. 71.

13. Richard D. Lyons, "Medicare's First Year: U.S. Reports Program Paid Out $3.2-Billion to Cover Doctor and Hospital Bills," *New York Times*, October 25, 1967, p. 28.

14. Ibid.

15. William A. Pearman and Philip Starr, *Medicare: A Handbook on the History and Issues of Health Care Services for the Elderly* (New York: Garland Publishing, 1988), p. 12.

16. Barbara Dreyfuss, "Twenty Years Later: Key Players Reminisce," *The Internist*, March 1985, p. 11.

17. HCFA, *Health Care Financing Review/1998 Statistical Supplement*, 1998, p. 46.

18. Normandy Brangan and Mary Jo Gibson, *FYI: The Cost of Prescription Drugs: Who Needs Help?* (Washington: AARP Public Policy Institute, 2000), p. 1.

19. Sheel M. Pandya et al., *Nursing Homes* (Washington: AARP Public Policy Institute, 2001).

20. U.S. Senate Committee on Finance (106-1), *Medicare Matters: The Value of Social Insurance*, Testimony of Marilyn Moon, The Urban Institute, May 27, 1999.

21. HCFA, *Health Care Financing Review: Medicare and Medicaid Statistical Supplement, 1999*, Publication 03417, November 1999, p. 129.

22. HCFA, *Health Care Financing Review/1998 Statistical Supplement*, p. 48.

23. Pandya et al.

24. Ibid.

25. Testimony before the U.S. Senate Special Committee on Aging (105-2), Janemarie Mulvey and Barbara Stucki, "Who Will Pay for the Baby Boomers' Long-Term Care Needs? Expanding the Role of Private Long-Term Care Insurance," American Council of Life Insurance, March 9, 1998, p. 4.

26. Testimony before the U.S. Senate Finance Committee, General Accounting Office, "Long-Term Care: Baby Boom Generation Increases Challenge of Financing Needed Services," Statement of William J. Scanlon, GAO-01-563T, March 27, 2001.

27. Barbara Coleman, *New Directions for State Long-Term Care Systems* (Washington: AARP Public Policy Institute, 1998), p. 1.

28. General Accounting Office, "Long-Term Care."

29. Richard D. James and Frank Morgan, "Patients Wanted: Surplus of Beds Puts Many Nursing Homes in Financial Difficulty," *Wall Street Journal*, March 25, 1965, p. 1.

30. U.S. House Committee on Ways and Means, *National Health Insurance Resource Book* (Washington: Government Printing Office, 1974), pp. 107–111.

31. Frank L. Schick and Renee Schick, eds., *Statistical Handbook on Aging Americans* (Phoenix: The Oryx Press, 1994), p. 242.

32. National Institute on Aging, National Institutes of Health, "New Census Report Shows Exponential Growth in Number of Centenarians," Press Release, June 16, 1999.

33. Louis S. Reed, *Research Report No. 10: The Extent of Health Insurance Coverage in the United States*, U.S. Department of Health, Education, and Welfare. Social Security Administration, Division of Research and Statistics (Washington: Government Printing Office, 1965), p. 23.

34. Robert Tanner, "Nursing-Home Neglect Rampant," Associated Press, August 7, 1999.

35. General Accounting Office, "Nursing Homes: Stronger Complaint and Enforcement Practices Needed to Better Assure Adequate Care," Statement of William J. Scanlon before the Senate Special Committee on Aging (106-1), March 22, 1999, GAO/T-HEHS-99-89.

36. Tanner.

37. Sheri I. David, *With Dignity: The Search for Medicare and Medicaid* (Westport, Conn.: Greenwood Press, 1985), p. 148.

38. Charlotte Twight, "Medicare's Origin: The Economics and Politics of Dependency," *Cato Journal* 16, no. 3 (Winter 1997): 319.

39. General Accounting Office, "Medicare: Lessons Learned from HCFA's Implementation of Changes to Benefits," GAO/HEHS-00-31, January 2000, p. 3.

40. U.S. Senate Committee on Finance (106-1), Mary Nell Lehnhard, Testimony of Blue Cross and Blue Shield Association, May 27, 1999.

41. U.S. Department of Health and Human Services, "Improper Fiscal Year 2000 Medicare Fee-for-Service Payments," A-17-00-02000, March 6, 2001.

42. Larry Margasak, "Medicare Contractors Implicated," Associated Press, July 13, 1999.

43. Robert Pear, "Fraud in Medicare Increasingly Tied to Claims Payers," *New York Times*, September 20, 1999, p. A1.

44. Ibid.

45. Ibid.

46. American Association of Retired Persons, *Your Three-Step Plan to Fight Medicare Fraud* (Washington: AARP, 1998).

47. Robert Moffit, "AAPS Report from Washington: Setback for Medicare Reform," *AAPS News* (Supplement), May 1999, p. S1.

48. Robert Moffit, "Official Washington's Continuing Assault on the Doctor-Patient Relationship," *F.Y.I.* (Washington: Heritage Foundation, 1997), Publication 161; Robert Moffit, *Answers to Frequently Asked Questions About Private Contracting in Medicare* (Fairfax, Va.: United Seniors Association, Inc., 1997).

49. *United Seniors Association, Inc., et al. v. Shalala*, 182 F.3d 965 (D.C. Cir. 1999). See also *Stewart v. Sullivan*, 816 F.Supp. 281 (D.N.J. 1992); John S. Hoff, *Medicare Private Contracting* (Washington: AEI Press, 1998).

50. HCFA, *Health Care Financing Review: Medicare and Medicaid Statistical Supplement*, 2000, pp. 226–228.

51. Robert Moffit, "HCFA's Latest Assault on Patient Privacy," *Executive Memorandum* (Washington: Heritage Foundation, 1999), Publication 580.

52. HCFA, November 20, 2000. See www.hcfa.gov/Medicaid/oasis/hhqcat02.htm. Accessibility verified July 14, 2001.

53. American Association for Homecare, Comments: Standards of Privacy of Individually Identifiable Health Information, March 30, 2001; 42 C.F.R 484.55; 64 Fed. Reg. 32984 (June 1999).

54. General Accounting Office, "Medicare: Improvements Needed to Enhance Protection of Confidential Health Information," Report to the Chairman, U.S. House Subcommittee on Health, Committee on Ways and Means, (106-1), GAO/HEHS-99-140, July 1999, p. 15.

55. Ibid., p. 18.

56. See the Health Insurance Portability and Accountability Act of 1996, Public Law 104-191, August 21, 1996.

57. "Standards for Privacy of Individually Identifiable Health Information," *Federal Register*, Vol. 65, No. 250, December 28, 2000, pp. 82461–82829; Sue Blevins and Robin Kaigh, *The Final Federal Medical Privacy Rule: Myths and Facts* (Washington: Institute for Health Freedom, 2001).

58. U.S. House Ways and Means Subcommittee (106-1), "Medicare Coverage Policy Determinations and Appeals," Testimony of Mike Hash, Deputy Administrator, Health Care Financing Administration, April 22, 1999.

59. The Hon. Jon Kyl (R-Ariz.), Kent Masterson Brown; J. Edward Hill, M.D.; and Robert E. Moffit, Ph.D., "Private Doctor-Patient Agreements: How the Medicare Law Forbids Free Choice," *Heritage Lectures* (Washington: Heritage Foundation, 1998), Publication 620, p. 12.

60. Joseph P. Newhouse and Gail R. Wilensky, "Paying for Graduate Medical Education: The Debate Goes On," *Health Affairs* 20, no. 2 (March/April 2001): 139.

61. Celinda Franco, "Medicare's Financing of Graduate Medical Education: Reforms and Issues," *CRS Report for Congress,* Congressional Research Service, Publication 96-491 EPW, 1998, p. CRS-1.

62. Ibid., p. CRS-6.

63. The Commonwealth Fund Task Force on Academic Health Centers, *Leveling the Playing Field: Financing the Missions of Academic Health Centers* (Boston: The Commonwealth Fund Task Force on Academic Health Centers, 1997).

Chapter 6

1. Melissa B. Jacoby, Teresa A. Sullivan, and Elizabeth Warren, "Medical Problems and Bankruptcy Filings," *Norton's Bankruptcy Adviser,* May 2000.

2. David Cutler and Louise Sheiner estimate that the first group (age cohort) of Medicare beneficiaries with any substantial payroll tax contributions, the 1910 cohort, had a "rate of return" of 28 percent. For the cohort of Medicare beneficiaries born around 1950 — the first to pay payroll taxes and income taxes throughout their life — the annual rate of return is expected to be 3.4 percent. For the 1980 cohort entering the labor force today, the rate of return is expected to be 2.2 percent. The returns on Medicare are higher than those for Social Security, but the Medicare return is falling over time. David M. Cutler and Louise Sheiner, *Generational Aspects of Medicare,* Federal Reserve Board, Finance and Economic Discussion Series, no. 2000-9, January 2000.

3. Meredith Bagby and Alden Levy, National Board Members of Third Millennium, Testimony before the National Bipartisan Commission on the Future of Medicare, April 21, 1998.

4. Spencer Rich and Judith Havemann, "As the Young Lose Faith in Medicare, Corporations Retreat on Health Coverage," *Washington Post*, October 9, 1996, p. A21.

5. Jennifer O'Sullivan, "Medicare: Prescription Drug Coverage for Beneficiaries," *CRS Report for Congress*, Congressional Research Service, Report RL30147, April 19, 1999, p. CRS-2.

6. Jack Hoadley, "Prescription Drug Coverage, Spending, Utilization, and Prices," Office of the Assistant Secretary for Planning and Evaluation, U.S. Department of Health and Human Services, April 20, 2001.

7. O'Sullivan; General Accounting Office, "Prescription Drugs: Increasing Medicare Beneficiary Access and Related Implications," Statement of David M. Walker, Testimony before the U.S. House Committee on Ways and Means, GAO/T-HEHS/AIMD-00-99, February 15, 2000.

8. U.S. House Committee on Ways and Means (107-1), Subcommittee on Health, *Laying the Groundwork for a Medicare Prescription Drug Benefit*, Testimony of Dan L. Crippen, March 27, 2001.

9. U.S. Senate Committee on Finance (106-1), *Prescription Drug Benefits and the Medicare Program*, Testimony of Dr. Morris B. Mellion, Blue Cross and Blue Shield Association, June 23, 1999.

10. Stephen Heffler et al., "Health Spending Growth Up in 1999; Faster Growth Expected in the Future," *Health Affairs* 20, no. 2 (March/April 2001): 197.

11. "New drugs" means new molecular entities approved by FDA. New molecular entities are drugs that have never been marketed in the United States. See Mellion.

12. Mellion.

13. Medicare Payment Advisory Commission, "Report to the Congress: Selected Medicare Issues," June 2000, p. 7

14. Crippen.

15. *A Blueprint for New Beginnings: A Responsible Budget for America's Priorities* (Washington: Government Printing Office, 2001), pp. 81–82, 186.

16. Crippen.

17. President's Framework to Strengthen Medicare, July 12, 2001, www.whitehouse.gov/news/releases/2001/07/20010712-3.html. Accessibility verified July 15, 2001.

18. Amy Goldstein, "Bush Has Pharmacy Discount Card Plan," *Washington Post*, July 11, 2001, p. A1.

19. Alan Greenspan, Board of Governors of the Federal Reserve System, Testimony before the National Bipartisan Commission on the Future of Medicare, April 20, 1998, p. 11.

20. The Federal Employees Health Benefits Program has been cited as a prototype for managed competition. See John C. Goodman and Gerald L. Musgrave, "A Primer on Managed Competition," NCPA Policy Report No. 183 (Dallas: National Center for Policy Analysis, 1994).

21. Memorandum titled "Medicare and FEHBP: A Basic Comparison," prepared by Beth Fuchs and Carolyn Merck, Specialists in Social Legislation, Congressional Research Service, Library of Congress, April 14, 1998.

22. Matthew Miller, "Premium Idea," *New Republic*, April 12, 1999.

23. Andrew J. Rettenmaier and Thomas R. Saving, *Pre-funding: A Solution to Medicare's Coming Financial Crisis*, Prepared for the U.S. House Joint Economic Committee, October 20, 2000; Andrew J. Rettenmaier and Thomas R. Saving, "Saving Medicare," *NCPA Policy Report*, No. 222 (Dallas: National Center for Policy Analysis, January 1999).

24. Rettenmaier and Saving, "Saving Medicare."

25. HCFA contracts under the Medicare program are for the most part statutorily exempt from the standard competitive bidding requirements imposed on other federal contracts (such as Defense Department contracts), although HCFA may choose to apply competitive bidding procedures. See 42 C.F.R. Section 421 (revised as of October 1, 2000); W. Bruce Shirk, "The Health Care Financing Administration's Contracting Authority under the Medicare Statute: An Overview," *Federal Contracts Report* (Washington: Bureau of National Affairs, 1997), pp. 778–785.

26. General Accounting Office, "Medicare: Higher Expected Spending and Call for New Benefit Underscore Need for Meaningful Reform," Statement of David M. Walker, Testimony before U.S. Senate Finance Committee (107-1), GAO-01-539T, March 22, 2001.

27. 42 C.F.R. Section 421; Shirk.

Index

Japan, 65, 66
Johnson Foundation, 59
Johnson, Lyndon Baines, 44, 46–47, 50, 58–59, 60, 74
Josiah Macy, Jr. Foundation, 111n25
Julius Rosenwald Fund, 111n25
Justice, Department of, 62, 76

Kaiser Foundation, 91
Kennedy, John F., 39, 40, 43–44, 45
Kerr-Mills law (Medical Assistance for the Aged (MAA) program), 20–22, 39–41, 47
Kerr, Robert, 39
King-Anderson Bill, 41, 43, 46, 47
King, Guy, 55
knowledge about Medicare, public lack of, ix, x, 1–23, 47–48, 53, 73, 75

laboratory services covered under Part B, 101
labor organizations, see unions
Lambert, Alexander, 27
largest world payer of health care, Medicare and Medicaid together as, viii, 4, 79
length of time beneficiaries remain in program, expected increase in, 12
liberal support for national health insurance, 17, 26, 32, 43
licensing
  monopoly power of medical profession and, 31
  prescription drugs, 31
life expectancy, x, 65–68, 74
Life Insurers Council, 42
long-term care, 9, 71–75, see also nursing home care, home care
long-term Medicare cost projections, 12–13, 15
lung cancer and tobacco, link between, 44
Luntz, Frank, 85
Luxembourg, 25

Macy Foundation, 111n25
Magnuson, Paul B., 37
male life expectancy at age 60, 67
managed care
  early attempts to use, 61
  early cost control measure, suggested as, 58
"managed competition" concept, 91–92

mandatory enrollment in Medicare, ix, x, 1–2, 10–12, 22, 25, 97–98, 107n33
  historical background to, see history of Medicare
  Medicaid and Medicare compared, 8
mandatory health insurance, see national health insurance, concept of
Marmor, Theodore, 37, 59
means testing
  Kerr-Mills program, under, 41
  Nixon's proposal for, 43
Medicaid
  AMA support for, 47
  compared to Medicare Parts A and B, 8
  creation of, ix, 46
  dual eligibility for Medicare and, 4
  "Eldercare" alternative to Medicare proposed by AMA as forerunner of, 46
  Kerr-Mills program, similarity to, 21, 22, 47
  life savings and qualification for, 75
  percentage of seniors qualifying for, 72
medical and related services
  Blue Shield plans, 10
  "Eldercare" proposal, coverage under, 45
  freeze on physician fees, attempt at, 62, 81
  Kerr-Mills program, coverage under, 41
  King-Anderson bill, no coverage under, 43
  Part B, coverage under, 5, 101, 102
  passage of Medicare linked to increase in physician fees, 58
  routine services not covered by Medicare, 102
Medical Assistance for the Aged (MAA) program (Kerr-Mills law), 20–22, 39–41
Medical Care for the American People (CCMC report, 1932), 29–35, 37
medical devices and equipment, 5, 99, 102
medical insurance, see health insurance
"medically necessary" requirement, 3, 95, 103
medical savings accounts (MSAs), 6, 94, 96
Medicare, see more specific entries

About the Author

Sue A. Blevins is founder and president of the Institute for Health Freedom, a nonpartisan, nonprofit think tank in Washington, D.C. She is a leading advocate and spokesman for consumers' freedom to choose their own health care. Blevins has appeared on numerous television and radio shows to discuss health care issues, and her articles have appeared in the *Wall Street Journal* and other publications. She is also the author of "Restoring Health Freedom: The Case for a Universal Tax Credit for Health Insurance" (Cato Policy Analysis no. 290), published by the Cato Institute.

Blevins developed her insights into health care systems through years of hands-on experience as a registered nurse in the United States and Canada. She received a master of public health degree from Harvard University and master of science and bachelor of science degrees from the Johns Hopkins University.

Cato Institute

Founded in 1977, the Cato Institute is a public policy research foundation dedicated to broadening the parameters of policy debate to allow consideration of more options that are consistent with the traditional American principles of limited government, individual liberty, and peace. To that end, the Institute strives to achieve greater involvement of the intelligent, concerned lay public in questions of policy and the proper role of government.

The Institute is named for *Cato's Letters*, libertarian pamphlets that were widely read in the American Colonies in the early 18th century and played a major role in laying the philosophical foundation for the American Revolution.

Despite the achievement of the nation's Founders, today virtually no aspect of life is free from government encroachment. A pervasive intolerance for individual rights is shown by government's arbitrary intrusions into private economic transactions and its disregard for civil liberties.

To counter that trend, the Cato Institute undertakes an extensive publications program that addresses the complete spectrum of policy issues. Books, monographs, and shorter studies are commissioned to examine the federal budget, Social Security, regulation, military spending, international trade, and myriad other issues. Major policy conferences are held throughout the year, from which papers are published thrice yearly in the *Cato Journal*. The Institute also publishes the quarterly magazine *Regulation*.

In order to maintain its independence, the Cato Institute accepts no government funding. Contributions are received from foundations, corporations, and individuals, and other revenue is generated from the sale of publications. The Institute is a nonprofit, tax-exempt, educational foundation under Section 501(c)3 of the Internal Revenue Code.

CATO INSTITUTE
1000 Massachusetts Ave., N.W.
Washington, D.C. 20001